Tarantulas

FROM THE EXPERTS AT
ADVANCED VIVARIUM SYSTEMS®

By Jerry G. Walls

THE HERPETOCULTURAL LIBRARY®
Advanced Vivarium Systems®
Irvine, California

Cover and book design concept by Michael Vincent Capozzi
Indexed by Kenneth Brace

Cover photo by Zig Leszczynski (front), and James Gerholdt (back).
Illustrations by Thomas Kimball.
The additional photographs in this book are by Isabelle Francais,
pp. 5, 14, 17, 20, 40, 43, 53, 63; James Gerholdt, pp. 6, 11, 13, 56, 57,
69, 77, 85, 87–89, 91; Paul Freed, 9, 19, 21, 22, 44, 45, 48, 55, 61, 68,
70, 71, 74, 76, 79, 80, 82; Maleta M. Walls, pp. 28, 29, 34, 35, 37, 67;
Zig Leszczynski, 72.

LCCN: 96-183295
ISBN: 1-882770-85-4
ISBN 13: 978-188277085-4

An Imprint of BowTie Press®
A Division of BowTie, Inc.
3 Burroughs
Irvine, CA 92618

We want to hear from you. What books would you like to see in the
future? Please feel free to write us with any comments on our AVS books.

Printed and bound in Singapore
10 9 8 7 6 5 4 3 2

CONTENTS

CHAPTER 1

GENERAL INFORMATION

Tarantulas! The very mention of these large, hairy spiders can bring chills of fear and disgust to many people and of course prompt the question, "Why on earth would you want to keep THAT as a pet?" The answer is that tarantulas are fascinating spiders that have intrigued naturalists and hobbyists for years, and they actually do very well as household pets.

For more than twenty-five years, the hobby of keeping tarantulas has been growing in numbers and in importance in the United States, Europe, and Japan. Today, it is possible to purchase specimens from about a hundred species from around the world, a quarter of these in the form of captive-bred young. Yet tarantulas still are misunderstood by many pet keepers and sellers; a surprising number, perhaps a quarter of those reaching the wholesaler, die each year from poor caging and from a misunderstanding of their basic needs. If kept properly, tarantulas can be excellent pets that are easy to care for and feed and that may (repeat, may) even breed in their cages.

This book is intended for beginners faced with making an initial purchase of the best tarantulas from a local shop or through the mail, learning how to house them correctly, and perhaps trying to satisfy their curiosity about how tarantulas breed and grow. It is not intended as a discussion of the complexities and uncertainties of tarantula taxonomy, though this subject must be touched upon so the hobbyist gains some idea of what type of tarantula he or she is considering to keep as a pet. It also is not a scientific treatise on tarantula anatomy and biology, though we will cover enough about these subjects in passing to put tarantulas in perspective. In fact, let's start with seeing just where tarantulas fit into the scheme of things and how they are related to other organisms.

Sight of this hairy tarantula crawling up a branch gives many people the creeps! However, tarantulas are in fact quite popular pets in households around the world. With an understanding of their needs, they're simple to care for and fun to observe.

Where Tarantulas Fit

Tarantulas are simply spiders—big and primitive spiders. They belong to the order Araneae (the spiders) of the phylum Arthropoda (invertebrate animals with jointed legs, including the insects, crustaceans, and even trilobites), and to the class Arachnida, a large assemblage of animals including such diverse groups as the scorpions, solpugids, and mites. Like insects and millipedes (class Insecta [also called class Uniramia] and class Myriopoda), they have jointed legs (four pairs in this case), but they don't have antennae (insects, millipedes, and centipedes have a single pair). The arachnids are among the most distinctive living invertebrates and have been around for hundreds of millions of years.

Spiders are themselves a group of at least thirty-five thousand species of minute to small invertebrates whose bodies are divided into just two parts: a large cephalothorax or prosoma comprising the head, mouthparts, and eyes, as well as the muscles that work the legs; and a generally rounded abdomen or opisthosoma that contains reproductive organs, breathing organs, the heart, kidneylike organs, and the silk glands, as well

as a major part of the digestive organs. The cephalothorax and abdomen are connected by a short, narrow tube—called the pedicel—through which pass the gut, blood sinuses, and nerves. Spiders are found virtually everywhere. There are probably at least a dozen species lurking around your kitchen right now, as well as another fifty species in your flower garden. Arachnologists divide the spiders into about one hundred smaller groups of closely related species; these groups are called families. Of these, about 15 percent comprise the primitive forms known all together as tarantulas and their allies, suborder Mygalomorphae.

Tarantulas overall are medium-sized, generally smooth spiders that have two large, projecting jaws called chelicerae (singular, chelicera), each ending in a slightly curved fang that is used to inject venom into the prey. The fang rotates up and down parallel to the center axis or plane of the body, whereas in most other spiders (advanced spiders, suborder Araneomorphae) the fangs are angled so when opened they are oblique or even perpendicular to the axis of the body. There is some indirect evidence that tarantulas were around as far back as four hundred million years, even before insects learned to fly.

Of the fifteen tarantula families, about half build tubular burrows capped with a door of thickened silk that can be rotated to allow the spider to reach out and grab passing prey. These trapdoor tarantulas often have a row of teeth (the rastellum) on the chelicerae that helps them dig their burrows. Most are small and are seldom seen, though some can be collected in the eastern United States as far north as Connecticut. A few species of the families Ctenizidae and Idiopidae are large enough to interest hobbyists.

The remaining families of tarantulas include generally small, smooth species with a variety of habits, but in the pet trade only the members of the family Theraphosidae (known as theraphosids)—the true or hairy tarantulas or bird spiders—are of great interest to pet keepers. Once called family Avicularidae, these generally are large spiders, commonly 1 ½ to 4 inches (3.8 to 10 centimeters) long, with projecting chelicerae, a rounded abdomen, and long hairs or bristles of many types on the legs and usually on the abdomen. Most true tarantulas burrow into the substrate or hide during the day under a shelter, but a few species are arboreal (tree-dwelling), building large masses of webs on trees and shrubs. For years literature has said that there are about eight hundred species of true tarantulas, but certainly by now the number must be closer to nine hundred, with perhaps several hundred more still to be defined by scientists. At least one hundred species appear in the hobby on occasion, but only twenty-five or fewer species form the core of the hobby—the species that are readily available to general hobbyists and beginners, that may be somewhat colorful or have distinctive behavior, and that can be kept with relative ease.

General Anatomy

Like other spiders, tarantulas have two major body divisions (the anterior cephalothorax, or prosoma, and the posterior abdomen, or opisthosoma) connected by a short stem or pedicel. They also have four pairs of walking legs, each ending in a pair of claws and all originating from the sternum under the cephalothorax. With very few exceptions, all spiders produce venom from long glands in the cephalothorax and/or chelicerae, but most are completely harmless to humans. Let's take a quick look at some of the more obvious parts of a tarantula's anatomy, especially the parts used for feeding and identification.

Top View

1. Tarsus
2. Metatarsus
3. Tibia
4. Patella
5. Femur
6. Chelicera
7. Pedipalp
8. Eye Tubercle
9. Cephalothorax
10. Abdomen
11. Spinnerets
12. Foveal Groove

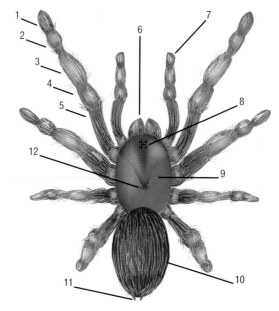

Bottom View

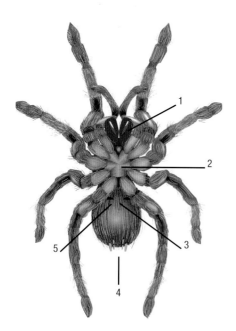

1. Fang
2. Sternum
3. Epigastric Ridge
4. Spinnerets
5. Book Lungs

Cephalothorax

The cephalothorax generally is round to oval in shape, usually with a nearly straight front edge. The topside of the cephalothorax is called the carapace, the underside the sternum. The eyes, eight in number, usually are positioned in two tight clusters atop a low tubercle just behind the center front edge of the carapace. Like most invertebrate eyes, they are simply clear spots in the exoskeleton that allow light to reach the retinal cells deeper within the cephalothorax. The

If you look closely, you can see the two eye clusters on top of this Brazilian black and white tarantula's head.

eyes of tarantulas are thought to detect movement rather than details of shape, and they function at short range—less than a foot (30 cm). Your tarantula may be able to detect your movements when you enter its cage, but it probably can't tell whether you are putting in your hand or a foot. An exception to this may be the arboreal tarantulas such as *Avicularia* spp., which can be active during the day and seem to have good vision that may allow them to distinguish one tarantula from another; it even has been suggested that they can see in color—most other tarantulas are night hunters (nocturnal) and would seem to lack color vision.

Near the center of the carapace is a deep groove or dimple that usually runs straight across the body but may be curved to the front or back, or even replaced by a tubercle. This is the foveal groove, which marks the point where several muscles originate and attach inside the cephalothorax. The shape and extent of this groove have been used as a taxonomic character, and the groove often is easy to detect, especially when the cephalothorax is only sparsely hairy.

The interior of the cephalothorax includes the front part of the digestive system as well as the brain, which is essentially a circle of large nerve cells behind the mouth and wrapped around the esophagus. It also houses the major muscles that attach the legs and pedipalps (see below) to the body, many of which attach to the sternum, the oval plate at the center of the underside of the cephalothorax.

Jaws and Pedipalps

The chelicerae project from the front center of the cephalothorax and each end in a dark, slightly curved, movable fang that is hollow and has a small opening on the underside just before the pointed tip. As mentioned, the fangs in tarantulas move up and down in the same axis as the center of the body, so they do not cross each other at the tips. The front upper edges of the chelicerae sometimes end in stout teeth that help the tarantula burrow; these teeth form the rastellum, which is not a common feature in pet tarantulas. In tarantulas, the venom glands are located almost strictly within the chelicerae and are relatively small. In more advanced spiders the venom glands are very large and occupy much of the front part of the cephalothorax.

Spiders do not have jaws in the same sense that humans and insects do, and they do not actually eat their prey. Instead, they salivate digestive juices over the prey until it becomes partially liquid and then suck in the juices, leaving the dry, hollow corpse; the body of the prey never enters the mouth of the spider. In tarantulas (and other spiders) the mouthparts are all outside the body and are parts of what look like short legs in front of the walking legs on each side—these "short legs" are the pedipalps. In some tarantulas, the pedipalps are large, hairy, and carry a color pattern similar to the pattern of their walking legs, so it is easy to mistake pedipalps for a fifth pair of legs. If you were to turn over a tarantula and look closely, however, you would see some obvious differences. Pedipalps have one segment fewer than a walking leg (lacking the metatarsus, which often is one of the longest leg segments) and end next to the body in widened plates called maxillae (or endites). These maxillae usually have tubercles or spines on their inner edges that are used to grind and soften hard prey so it can be more easily digested. The maxillae surround the opening to the mouth of the tarantula, which looks like a small hole surrounded by special bristles of several types that serve to strain out larger particles of the prey so they are not accidentally swallowed. The pedipalps are muscular and can help hold and manipulate dying or dead prey that has been struck by the fangs and is being bathed by digestive juices pumped out of the tarantula's mouth. Pedipalps also help soften the prey and move it around so all parts are digested and can be sucked into the mouth. If the pedipalps are injured near their bases, as during a bad molt, the tarantula may starve to death.

Pedipalps also are used as secondary sexual organs in spiders, and they are of different shapes in adult males and females. In a female spider or an immature specimen of either sex, the pedipalps usually end in claws like those

Spotted walking down a branch, this Antillean pink-toe tarantula's two short front "legs"—the pedipalps —are easily distinguished from its eight walking legs, which are each one segment longer than a pedipalp.

found on the walking legs. In an adult male, however, the end of the pedipalp (the tarsus) is modified into a sperm bulb to carry sperm to the female's reproductive system; it is modified to allow the sperm bulb to be protected when not in use and fully flexible when in use. We'll talk more about this in the breeding chapter.

Legs

The walking legs of most tarantulas are generally similar in shape and structure across the group, though the length of the pairs can vary greatly in different species. In fact, arachnologists have developed formulas to compare the lengths of the legs and the different parts of the legs of different species of tarantulas; these commonly are used in keys and species descriptions. Unfortunately, the measurements are almost impossible to make on a living tarantula and may not be accurate in a shed skin. Every walking leg has the same segments: a relatively short, squarish coxa at the base next to the sternum, followed by an even smaller trochanter; next comes a thick, long femur that sometimes is bowed, followed by a short patella or knee segment, the point of obvious flexing of a resting tarantula's leg; after this is a long tibia and an almost equally long metatarsus, followed by a shorter tarsus ending in a pair of claws (or, rarely, three claws).

Bristles

Taxonomists, scientists who try to recognize and describe the many species of animals and plants, often use a detailed examination of the types of bristles on the legs and body of a tarantula as a major method of telling species apart. There are hundreds of types of bristles on a tarantula that serve many functions (from defense to straining the "soup"). Of interest to identification are thickened bristles on the sides of the chelicerae that can rub against other special bristles on the pedipalps to produce a sound; this is a stridulatory organ (the sound produced by the friction may be at too high a frequency for humans to hear) and also may be present on the first walking legs. In some tarantulas, there are greatly

As this Brazilian salmon bird-eater tarantula consumes an anole, we get a close-up view of the spider's many sensory bristles on the legs. These are found in a great variety of sizes and thicknesses and serve many functions. They aid the spider in sensing predators and prey as well as possibly humidity and temperature in the substrate.

elongated bristles behind the mouth (sometimes called a beard) or on the edges of specific walking-leg segments. Someone once said that spider taxonomy (identification and naming) is a study of bristles, and they weren't far wrong.

Of very practical interest to hobbyists are special bristles found on the upper surface of the abdomen of most American tarantulas (Note: In this book, American tarantulas are species that come from the New World—North, Central, and South Americas as well as the Caribbean). These bristles are loosely attached to the body and can be brushed or kicked off by the back legs when a tarantula is angry or excited. Called urticating hairs, these bristles are barbed and bladed and quickly work their way under the surface of the skin of a predator—or into the hands and face of an incautious hobbyist. Though urticating hairs are not technically poisonous, they act like bits of fiberglass that cause extreme irritation of the skin and may cause local allergic reactions in the nose, eyes, and lips. The irritation soon goes away, but it's one that will be long remembered.

Abdomen

A tarantula's abdomen is simple in appearance—just a large, oval or slightly elongated bag of tough, flexible skin that may be densely or sparsely covered with bristles. Its underside shows only a few landmarks, including four rather

Looking closely at this African king baboon tarantula, you can see spun silk remnants attached to the large pair of spinnerets.

squarish raised areas near the front; sometimes partially hidden by the last pair of legs, these are the book lungs, which are used for breathing. Between the front pair of book lungs is a ridge, the epigastric furrow, that includes the opening to the internal sex organs. At the end of the abdomen are two or three pairs of spinnerets (one pair being generally much longer than the others) from which silk is spun to line the burrow, to form draglines when a tarantula jumps or moves from its burrow, and to wrap prey for digestion, as well as many other essential tasks. The anus lies above the spinnerets, often on a small mound.

Inside the abdomen are most of the major organs of a tarantula. Most important, perhaps, is the heart, which is a long tube positioned down the center line of the top of the abdomen. It is sometimes visible through the skin (cuticle) when a tarantula scrapes all the bristles from its abdomen. The heart is a pump with paired openings on its sides; it helps push blood (technically, hemolymph in a spider and based on copper rather than on iron, as is vertebrate blood) through the cavities or sinuses of the entire body. A tarantula does not have arteries, veins, and capillaries as found in vertebrate animals; instead, the blood is dispersed through the entire body and simply flows at low pressure around all the organs and muscles; this is why a tarantula quickly bleeds to death if it suffers an injury that breaks the cuticle.

Also in the abdomen are the major portion of the intestines, large organs that serve as kidneys, and most of the reproductive system (testes in males and ovaries in females). The silk glands occupy a significant part of the abdominal cavity in most tarantulas.

The entire body of a tarantula is covered with a tough, often inflexible "skin" more properly called the cuticle; this forms the exoskeleton. The muscles attach to the underside of the exoskeleton, which may be supplied with a variety of bumps and expansions to allow muscles to work as effective levers and apply great strength to the legs and other movable parts. The cuticle is largely a complex sugar (formally, chitin) that can become quite hard when the calcium salts within it are exposed to the air. This is how the soft skin of a newly molted tarantula becomes hardened after a few hours or days. It also explains why a newly molted tarantula is virtually unable to walk, because the internal attachment points of the muscles are shed with the outer skin, and the new attachments are also soft at first.

Basic Natural History

Obviously, different tarantula species may have quite different biologies—you would not expect a desert dweller to live quite the same way as one that lives in palm trees in the rain forest. The following information is just the tip of the iceberg when dealing with tarantula natural history. Look for details in the breeding chapter and the section on molting in the health maintenance chapter.

Range

Most true (or theraphosid) tarantulas (the families of smaller tarantulas may have much wider distributions) are found in the tropics and subtropics of the Americas, Africa, and Asia, though some species extend northward to Colorado in the western United States and south almost to Patagonia in South America. A few species are found in southern Europe and several unusual species are found in New Guinea and Australia. In the United States, true tarantulas are found from central California northeast to

Colorado, and through Arkansas and southern Missouri, and south through Louisiana; with most species found from Texas to Southern California in deserts and dry prairie habitats. Numerous species of true tarantulas, many new to the hobby market, are found in dry habitats from central Mexico to central South America, as are some arboreal and rain forest species. Africa and southern Asia (including southern China and Indonesia) have many tarantula species, though relatively few enter the American market.

Habitat

As a rule, tarantulas are secretive ground dwellers (terrestrial) that spend their lives in burrows in suitable soil or in shallow depressions (scrapes) under dead trees and other debris. As you already know, there are exceptions to this, because quite a few tarantulas are arboreal, living all or most of their lives in shrubs or even tall trees where they use thick webs to protect themselves and help assure that they have sufficient humidity to function.

A tarantula's life is in many respects connected more to humidity than to food or even to mating. Tarantulas dehydrate easily, and even the species from the driest deserts need a constant source of moisture around them during most of their lives. The burrows provide tarantulas with safe retreats that help conserve moisture when properly placed in soils that seldom dry out completely. This is one reason that tarantulas often are found in colonies or at least in concentrations where the soils can be dug into to form stable burrows and where the vegetation prevents winds and sunlight from drying out the area too quickly before the next rains come.

On the other hand, tarantulas seldom burrow in low areas that are subject to flooding, because they can drown if trapped in a burrow when water rises and submerges their book lungs, which are at the front of the underside of the abdomen. The lungs function by oozing hemolymph through the many very thin, flat plates in each lung that have one surface exposed to the air, allowing oxygen to be absorbed and carbon dioxide to be released.

Feeding

All tarantulas are carnivorous, and they feed on living prey. Most tarantulas seem to prefer small insects and other invertebrates that don't put up much of a fight when caught, which means the tarantulas get dinner by expending very little energy. Even the largest tarantulas would prefer to

An orange baboon (also called an African orange starburst) tarantula camps out in its web. This spider's aggressiveness may make it a poor choice for beginning tarantula keepers, but its bold color and high contrasting abdominal markings continue to increase its popularity among advanced hobbyists and dealers.

take half a dozen nearly defenseless crickets rather than have to fight with a single armored beetle that weighs the same as the combined weight of the crickets. There are indeed records of wild tarantulas actually taking nestling birds and small rodents from their nests, as well as the occasional lizard, frog, and even small snake, but these are exceptions to the usual rule. Some tarantulas will take animals that have recently died, but in most cases they can only detect food when it moves, so a dead cricket will be ignored unless the mouth of the tarantula is actually placed over it. (This sometimes is done with very ill tarantulas that can only eat squashed, freshly killed crickets.) The fangs inject a neurotoxin that can kill prey up to the size of a mouse but generally is harmless to humans. A very large tarantula has

17

tremendous force in its chelicerae, however, and can drive a fang through a human fingernail.

Digestion takes place outside the body, with the spider regurgitating strong digestive juices on the prey, which usually is wrapped in silk to help control it and also to store it for later meals. Remember, the tarantula does not actually swallow its food—what you see left in the terrarium are empty husks of crickets with all their soft tissues digested away. If you feed a very juicy morsel, such as a pinky mouse (a newborn mouse before its eyes open), to a tarantula, the spider will treat it just like a cricket, including mangling it by the maxillae of the pedipalps and producing a truly bloody mess. The remains will be shriveled skin bits with some cartilage and other indigestible parts.

Tarantulas feed at night, as a rule, generally waiting for prey to wander near the opening of the burrow or scrape and trip a fine silk line that warns the spider that prey is near. When motion is detected close enough (less than a body length, usually) to the tarantula, the spider rapidly moves from the burrow, grabs the prey with its pedipalps and front legs, and injects it with venom that kills it or at least slows its heartbeat enough to prevent struggling. The prey may be eaten immediately or, if food is abundant, wrapped in silk and stored for later. A tarantula will feed until it is sated and will ignore prey if it is already full. Because of the low energy requirements of a tarantula, it needs little food, and an adult female tarantula may reproduce and survive on only a few insect meals each month during the active season.

Growth and Reproduction

Tarantulas grow slowly by molting their old cuticle and replacing it with a fresh cuticle. The number of molts varies greatly with age, sex, temperature, humidity, feeding, and probably species. As a rule, rapidly growing young tarantulas molt a dozen or more times during their first year, reducing the number of molts as they grow until adulthood when they may molt only once or twice a year or perhaps only once every two years. Males mature much sooner than females do and molt fewer times. Males also die at a much younger age than females do. Some female burrowing tarantulas may live more than twenty years in nature and in captivity, whereas few males live longer than six to eight years. Curiously, arboreal tarantulas may have much shorter lives than burrowers, perhaps because they live without going through seasonal periods of inactivity and are active all their lives (compared with burrowers from northern climates that may spend only a few months of each year actively feeding); few female tree-dwelling tarantulas live longer than ten years.

Males usually hunt out females for mating by visiting them in their burrows or arboreal retreats. Because females may mistake males for food, tarantulas have developed structural and behavioral adaptations to allow safe mating, which we'll discuss later. Females usually lay many small eggs in a silken egg case, which they protect until tiny spiderlings are hatched. The spiderlings generally are almost smooth and bear little resemblance to the parents in shape, color, or general appearance. The spiderlings quickly disperse before they are eaten by a sibling or the mother, and each forms its own tiny burrow and catches its own prey. There is little or no family life in tarantulas. (However, some trapdoor tarantulas allow the young to remain in the mother's burrow for several years and even share their mother's prey.)

This Antillean pink-toe juvenile is just barely the size of a human fingertip. It will grow to a 2-inch (5-cm) adult body length, its bright blue hue changing to pinks, reds, and greens with each molt.

CHAPTER 2

SELECTION

F inding the perfect tarantula can be difficult, as many commonly imported species (especially from Africa and Asia) are simply too aggressive to make good pets for the beginning or intermediate keeper. The most colorful American tarantulas tend to be expensive, but if you can find affordable half-grown to adult specimens, they probably make the best pets. Tiny spiderlings are less expensive but harder to care for. After you have become used to caring for a grown tarantula, you may find it easier to care for spiderlings. First, however, let's try to relieve your fears about whether it truly is safe to own a tarantula as a pet.

The Deadly Tarantula?

Tradition has branded tarantulas as venomous killers that would not hesitate to attack a human. This idea has been around for at least three hundred years and is widespread in novels, movies, television, and even some scientific books. (The most widely used book on identifying North American spiders erroneously mentions the "deadly bite" of

With more than one hundred tarantula species available for purchase, you certainly should be able to find a pet with a temperament that fits your experience level and an appearance that suits your aesthetic desires.

some South American tarantulas.) The reality is quite different, because tarantulas are shy, secretive animals that certainly wouldn't attack something the size of a human unless cornered with no way to escape. Yes, laboratory tests do show that for some reason tarantula venom is especially toxic to small mice and rats, and this has been taken as evidence that a bite may be dangerous to humans. Humans are not mice, fortunately, and experience proves that the bites of most (but not all) tarantulas are fairly harmless.

Exceptions occur, however, and there is good reason to believe (though actual scientific evidence is sparse) that American tarantulas belonging to the genera *Acanthoscurria, Theraphosa, Phormictopus, Tapenauchenius,* and *Lasiodora* could cause more widespread reactions, including shortness of breath and swelling of an arm, for more than a day. These also happen to be generally aggressive spiders that do not fail to defend themselves if approached.

Species of genus *Lasiodora* are typically too aggressive to recommend for beginning tarantula keepers. These terrestrial spiders don't spend as much time in their burrows as other tarantulas do, making them a good choice for experienced hobbyists who want to readily observe their pets.

Even more potentially dangerous are many or most tarantulas from Africa and Asia. Though none of the species in the hobby are certain to have caused major human problems, the ornamental tarantulas (*Poecilotheria* spp.) of India and Sri Lanka have certainly caused severe shortness of breath and uneven heartbeats, reportedly resulting in hospitalization. The large earth tigers of southern Asia (*Haplopelma* spp.) are reputed to be just as bad. In Africa,

Another aggressive species is the unicorn or straight-horned baboon spider (*Ceratogyrus cornuatus*). These large tarantulas are easily recognized by the horn on the carapace.

the feather-legged tarantulas (*Stromatopelma* spp.) are greatly feared, and there is some evidence that their venom can affect the human heart. Similarly, the very aggressive baboon spiders of southern Africa (*Citharischius* spp., *Ceratogyrus* spp., and *Pterinochilus* spp.) are reputed to cause more than temporary swelling and numbness from their bites and have close relatives (*Harpactirella* spp.) that are *said* to have killed humans.

It is fairly certain that the release of venom is under voluntary control of the spider, and only a few bites to predators (meaning you) are likely to release a significant amount of venom. This makes it even harder to determine whether a tarantula truly is dangerous to humans, as anecdotal evidence from even many bites doesn't prove that the venom has had a chance to act. Play it safe if you plan to keep any of these tarantulas; keep their cages securely covered and locked and never handle the spiders.

Are tarantulas deadly? No, probably not. Are they dangerous? Yes, just a few. Make sure to consider the danger potential when choosing a pet tarantula. Your best choices for a "safe" tarantula certainly would be a Mexican red-knee (*Brachypelma smithi*) or painted red-leg (*Brachypelma emilia*), followed by any other *Brachypelma* species. North American *Aphonopelma* species and Chilean rose tarantulas (*Grammostola rosea*) probably are safe, as are the pink-toes (*Avicularia* spp.), if you have enough experience to take care of fast-moving spiders. Of Old World tarantulas, the starburst tarantulas (*Pterinochilus* spp.) may be safe, though there have been a few reports of localized reactions to bites. Anecdotal evidence casts doubt on the safety of other tarantulas.

Bites and Allergies

If your tarantula bites you, which is likely only if you try to handle it or are careless when cleaning the cage, you could suffer some pain and possible bleeding because the tarantula basically has driven small nails into your hand. The pain soon passes, but the area around the bite may become red and slightly swollen, and there may be a numbing tingle in the hand or adjacent fingers for a few hours to a day. Keep the wound iced and apply an antibiotic salve to prevent secondary infections. That's usually about it—no fingers falling off, no heart attacks, no need for a visit to the emergency room. This applies to almost all common pet tarantulas, especially the species of *Aphonopelma, Brachypelma, Avicularia,* and *Grammostola* found in pet shops.

If you are bitten by one of the potentially dangerous South American, African, or Asian tarantulas, it would be wise to spend the rest of the day just reading or watching TV and avoiding exercise that could spread venom. If you feel any shortness of breath or notice an irregular heartbeat, have someone calmly drive you to an emergency room for observation. Almost certainly nothing will happen, but one never knows for sure. Individual reactions to any venom (from bees to rattlesnakes) vary greatly, and self-induced hysteria over the potential danger of a bite could be worse than the venom itself. Remember, there is no hard evidence that any tarantula in captivity has actually killed anyone, and most bites don't even inject any venom (so-called dry bites).

Avoid speculative treatment for bites. At the moment, there is no antidote for a venomous bite and very little evidence to show that one is needed. There also is no real evidence that the venom of a big *Theraphosa* spp. is the same as that of a feather-leg or that either would react well to injections of widow spider (*Latrodectus* spp.) antivenin. Treatment, if any, presumably would have to be supportive to stabilize breathing and heartbeat. I'm not aware of any such treatment ever being needed in the United States, though thousands of people keep tarantulas, including many of the potentially dangerous species, and bites are not uncommon. An allergy is a different story and one whose course cannot be predicted. It is quite possible that you could have an allergic reaction (anaphylactic shock) to even a small amount of venom from a harmless tarantula, much as some people react badly to a bee sting. An allergic reaction assumedly could include a rash, itching, shortness of breath, and collapse. Anaphylactic shock can be treated in familiar ways in any emergency room, but again I'm not aware any cases in the United States.

You are much more likely to develop localized and sometimes dangerous rashes from the urticating hairs on the abdomens of many common American tarantulas. The species of *Aphonopelma* and *Brachypelma*, among others, are notorious for kicking thick clouds of bristles off their abdomens with a hind leg, and the webs of *Avicularia* species are notoriously bristle-laden. *Pseudotheraphosa* spp. and *Theraphosa* spp. hairs can cause extensive bleeding sores on humans. The cages of any of these tarantulas may be coated inside with urticating hairs, which could be breathed in each time you open the cage. Then the bristles can work their way into your nose, lips, and mouth, where they cause irritation to mucous tissues with swelling and redness. If a tarantula sprays you with bristles, many could become embedded in the tissues around your eye (or even in the eye itself), causing painful swelling and even temporary blindness until the eye is cleaned by a doctor. A child holding a tarantula next to the face could be in serious, though temporary, trouble. Hand-washing is a must after handling tarantulas and their cages.

There are many anecdotal reports of keepers developing allergies to urticating hairs and being forced to give up their tarantulas or face repeated hospital treatment, and some perhaps are true. There is little doubt that irritation from these bristles can be painful and annoying, and if present in large numbers, the bristles could cause serious eye and

throat problems (possibly blocking the air passages or causing blindness). It seems that the bristles do not carry any
toxins, so the damage they cause is strictly physical, a result
of the barbs having worked their way into the tissues; this
means that true allergic reactions are not likely, though certainly not impossible. Rashes on the hands and arms are
commonly treated with hydrocortisone creams, whereas
affected eyes may need special rinses under the guidance of
a doctor. Urticating hairs are not something to ignore if you
believe you could have stronger than normal reactions to
everyday activities involving your tarantula.

Captive-Bred Versus Wild-Caught

Many tarantulas have small geographic ranges and probably
don't occur in large numbers in the wild. They also face the
usual problems tropical animals do, including loss of suitable habitat due to conversion of forests to pastures and
savannas to villages, as well as total flooding of huge areas by
hydroelectric dams. Add to this a sometimes massive collecting of attractive species for the pet trade, and you can
understand why some tarantula species have become greatly
reduced in numbers in the wild. Even in the United States,
where native tarantulas are not that popular as pets, large
numbers lose their homes to land conversion, and ines-
timable numbers of males are killed each year by automo-
biles as they cross roads while looking for females.

In 1985, the Convention on International Trade in
Endangered Species (CITES) listed the very popular and
colorful Mexican red-knee tarantula (*Brachypelma smithi*)
under Appendix II, which effectively allowed Mexico to pro-
hibit exportation of the species and its relatives while receiv-
ing cooperation from the United States and other countries
that recognized the CITES treaty (http://www.cites.org).
Red-knees virtually disappeared from the market except for
those smuggled out of Mexico (a practice that continues
even today) and older specimens already established in col-
lections. Fortunately, this species has females that live for
more than twenty years in captivity and breed fairly easily,
so within a few years the first tiny captive-bred spiderlings

became available for sale. They sold at higher prices than adults had sold a few years earlier, but they found a good market and became an incentive for many breeders to try their hand at captive breeding a variety of tarantulas. Today, perhaps about twenty-five species are bred on a regular basis, with spiderlings available for just a few dollars even when very expensive imported adults are available.

By all means, start with captive-bred tarantulas of one of the common species (see chapter 6). The most common ones generally are also the most attractive and docile, and they make the best pets until you gain more experience. Captive-breds usually are healthy, are of known age, and often have been sexed by experts based on details of their shed skins. Imports may be dehydrated and carry bacterial infections and intestinal worms; little may be known about how to establish them in the terrarium.

Unfortunately, the cheapest spiderlings are tiny and look nothing like the adults; they might be hard to tell from spiders you notice around the house. Each spiderling needs its own small cage and careful feeding. It grows slowly, with the males often taking three to five years to mature and females taking six to eight years. They may not resemble the adults until they are three or four years old. However, you can house many different species in a small area and spend relatively little money for what, with patience, will become a great collection of beautiful adults.

Recognizing a Sick Tarantula

If you buy a small spiderling, you probably are going to have to depend on the experience of the seller or breeder as to whether it is healthy or not. But if you are interested in an imported or captive-bred spider that is half grown to adult, then you can at least get an idea if the animal is healthy. Healthy tarantulas are shy, but they are obviously alert—they tend to lurk at the front of their burrows or hiding spots, ready to duck back in if threatened or emerge to snap up food. They never just lie exposed in a corner with their legs tucked under their body—such a tarantula is sick and likely to die in a few days.

Don't worry about bare patches on top of the abdomen in American tarantulas—these just represent where the tarantula has swept away the urticating hairs. After the spider molts (usually within a year if adult), the bristles will return in all their irritating glory. If the end of a leg is missing or deformed, this also may not make much difference once the tarantula eventually molts and replaces the leg. Sometimes you can get "slightly defective" tarantulas for a bargain price, and they often make good, long-lived pets. Sometimes, of course, they die of complications during their molt, the decision is yours.

Never buy a tarantula that is not eating. You can look for dried cricket or mealworm husks in the cage (though hopefully the seller has made an effort to clean the cage), or you can ask that the tarantula be fed a cricket so you can see it eat. Be aware that not every tarantula eats every week, especially older adults, so you may have to come back later when the tarantula is more interested in food.

The Male Problem

The usual suggestion is to not buy an adult male tarantula because males usually die in six months to two years from when they become sexually mature. Unfortunately, many tarantulas are collected when roaming the roads, and these are almost always males looking for females. Males tend to be high-strung, as their little brains are overwhelmed by desires of mating; their only goal is to find a female and mate. They may not eat and may burn great amounts of energy just continually moving around the terrarium looking for a way out.

You will have to pay more for sexed young female tarantulas, as they have long lives to live—many species have females that can live twenty years or more. Young males (sexed correctly at least two years before they have their final molt and become sexually mature) can make good pets if reasonably priced, but take them with the knowledge that they will not live as long as females will. Of course, if you are not really willing to be saddled with a female tarantula for twenty years, a young male might make an excellent pet for a few years.

Handling a Tarantula

I realize that many books tell you to never handle your tarantula, and undoubtedly this is the best thing for the spider. Tarantulas are easily injured if dropped, as they can rupture their abdomen and bleed to death. Even a very tame tarantula can become excited or scared while being handled and make an abrupt leap or run for freedom, sometimes biting before leaping to its death on a hard floor. American tarantulas that are handled will often retaliate by spraying the handler with urticating hairs. Certainly it is best to not handle your tarantula. Instead, if you wish to move it from one area to another, shoo it into a plastic tumbler or clear plastic box, hold a piece of cardboard over the top, and quickly carry it to where you want it to go.

Using a cup or bottle to move a tarantula prevents accidents—to the tarantula and to you!

However, almost all beginners want to at least occasionally handle their tarantulas. If you stick to the most docile species, such as the Mexican red-knee and painted red-leg or the Chilean rose, you can handle many specimens. The best way to pick one up is to cup it with both hands from the sides and then roll your palms over so the tarantula is free to move around a bit when one hand is removed. Most will head for a higher spot, such as your shoulder or head, which can be a problem. Whatever you do, do it steadily, don't hesitate, and make sure the spider knows you are getting ready to pick it up. Tarantulas don't like surprises. Never allow your fingers to come into contact with the fangs—that is just too much of a risk. Always hold the tarantula over a soft surface, such as carpet; and never hold it higher than a few inches, in case it falls. If you are bitten (even the most tame tarantula may bite occasionally) or your pet has an accident, don't blame me—I recommended using a tumbler, remember.

Cover the cup with a plate as shown here to keep the tarantula contained.

CHAPTER 3

HOUSING AND FEEDING

Tarantulas are among the easiest pets to care for, but even they have certain basic housing and feeding requirements that must be met if they are to thrive. If you remember that almost all tarantulas are adapted to living in a relatively humid burrow or web environment at stable temperatures, you should have no problems with at least the common species.

Humidity

In nature, tarantulas live in stable environments that they rarely leave voluntarily except at night. A tarantula's burrow serves to conserve moisture, and the placement of the burrow helps the tarantula regulate its temperature. By digging into the soil or utilizing a preexisting rodent burrow (many common tarantulas lack the strong spines on the chelicerae and the legs that would allow them to dig into hard soils), a tarantula enters a world that is cooler and more humid than at the surface. Think of desert tarantulas; they live in colonies that take advantage of the porous nature of local soils and may dig down several feet until the proper humidity and temperature are reached. Once a burrow is established by a spiderling, the spider keeps modifying its retreat as the spider grows. Eventually, there may be several side tunnels and resting chambers beyond the primary opening where the tarantula usually lurks, waiting for food to stroll by. When tarantulas leave their burrows, it generally is on relatively humid nights, and females seldom wander more than a few feet away from their retreats. One reason males live short lives in nature is that, when they become roamers in search of females, they must utilize temporary hiding places during the day, and they almost certainly are subject to dehydration as well as more predation.

You can assume that all tarantulas need a relative humidity of about 65 percent in their retreats, whether a burrow or under an overturned partial flowerpot. This level may vary within about 5 to 10 percent in either direction. Species known to come from very humid tropical habitats, such as the curly-hair (*Brachypelma albopilosum*), need higher humidity in the retreat, so give them a chance to look for a relative humidity of nearly 80 percent.

Humidity Gradients

Remember that 65 percent is the suggested humidity of the *retreat*, not necessarily the entire terrarium. In fact, it probably is best to give the tarantula a humidity gradient, much as we give reptiles and amphibians a temperature gradient to allow the animals to thermoregulate. The burrow area should be most humid, with perhaps an area at the far side of the cage at only 50 percent humidity. Keep an eye on your pet and notice its movements. If the tarantula spends much of its time in a relatively dry region, then the humidity in the area you've selected for the retreat may be too high, so allow it to dry somewhat. If the spider spends all its time on and near the water dish, the retreat and perhaps the entire terrarium may be too dry, so you should change substrate type, or add more water to the substrate at least near the retreat. Excessive humidity can be just as disabling as dry conditions.

Measuring Humidity

Relative humidity is measured with an instrument called a hygrometer (no, not a hydrometer, which measures specific gravity of liquids). In the past, hygrometers were bulky, expensive machines that certainly were not usable in terrarium conditions. Today, many companies offer fairly accurate hygrometers that are inexpensive and can be used to measure relative humidity—not only an inch (2.5 cm) or so above the center of the terrarium (the ambient relative humidity of a terrarium), but also within or at least very near the retreat itself (the specific relative humidity). My personal favorite is a combined electronic thermometer and hygrometer that provides you with two measurements:

one at the readout itself and the other from a small remote probe that can be placed in or near the burrow. With the flick of a switch, you can register the temperature and humidity of the burrow and rest assured that you are giving your pet enough substrate humidity to keep it comfortable. These units are small (many about 2 inches x 3 inches [5 x 7.5 cm]), thin, work a long time on a battery, and are very affordable. They can be found in most electronic parts stores as well as in mass market stores. My suggestion would be to place the unit next to the terrarium (outside, otherwise it will be covered with webbing) at about the same level as the water dish and to run the probe down into the substrate as close to under the retreat as possible. Remember that tarantulas may climb cords to escape, so be sure that where the cord enters the cage is securely sealed; use a silicone plug if necessary.

Temperature

Though many common tarantulas come from dry, hot desert and savanna areas, high temperatures are not desirable when keeping tarantulas. In fact, temperatures much higher than 86 degrees Fahrenheit (30 degrees Celsius) make the tarantula uncomfortable (causing stress) and increase dehydration; they can lead to a quick death or a week of stress and then death.

Burrows and retreats are relatively humid and thus cooler than the surrounding surface, plus the substrate itself helps insulate the spider from extremes of temperatures. In nature the tarantula's burrow usually is situated in a shaded or partially shaded area where vegetation or rocks help divert drying winds, increasing humidity and decreasing temperature. Most keepers contend that their captive-kept tarantulas do best in a terrarium with an ambient temperature of roughly 70°F–85°F (21°C–29.4°C), which thankfully is about the same as common room temperatures. This means that all common terrestrial tarantulas can be kept without additional heating in most homes. Tarantulas also can survive quite well when the retreat temperature drops to as little as 60°F (15.5°C), though they become sluggish and won't feed.

Remember, this is the temperature in the retreat, not the ambient cage temperature.

Use a thermometer to measure the temperature both in the center of the terrarium (ambient) and the retreat (specific). Don't just guess; few people can accurately judge temperatures, especially in the high relative humidity in a retreat.

Extra Heat

If extra heat is needed (indicated by a tarantula becoming sluggish and curling up in the warmest area of the terrarium), you can try using a small undertank heating pad under a third of the cage floor away from the retreat. Never place heating pads under the entire floor, as this could force a burrowing tarantula to try to make its retreat in an area of excessive heat, leading to stress and death. Be sure all heaters (pads, strips) are correctly installed and not subject to dangerous shorts that could lead to fires.

Keep tarantula terraria away from air conditioners and heating vents; I'm not aware of tarantulas being able to catch respiratory viruses ("colds"), but certainly they are not adapted to moving warm or cold air.

If you need just a little bit of extra heat for a terrarium during the winter, try using a small (15 watts maximum) incandescent red lightbulb over the cage. A bulb larger than this can lead to excessive heat and dehydration. The red color will allow you to watch your pet as it moves around during the night. Never place a bulb *within* the cage, as it could easily cause burns when the tarantula crawls over it and covers it with webbing. Be very careful whenever offering extra heat to a tarantula—make sure your thermometer is working well and is placed so you know the specific temperature in the retreat, which must not exceed 86°F (30°C).

Basic Terrarium Setups

Once you understand the humidity and temperature needs of a tarantula, it becomes rather easy to keep it happy. Tarantulas are not intelligent animals and have very static lifestyles: they spend the day in their burrows, leave their retreat at night to snag prey, defecate on occasion, and drink from a water bowl. That's it, nothing fancy. Don't expect them to greet you when you come home as a dog would.

Cage

Start by considering that only one tarantula can be safely housed in a single terrarium. If you place two tarantulas in a cage, one will kill the other, often the day or two following the first molt when the body is soft and the spider is defenseless. One tarantula, one cage. (Exceptions occur with the tree-dwellers, which we'll discuss later in this chapter.) Tarantulas don't need or want large cages—they are used to tight burrows and retreats and can get lost in a large cage, unable to find their food and water. You also don't need a very high cage; it would encourage a tarantula to climb up to corners where it could fall long distances, which is dangerous. For virtually all common tarantulas (except the very largest, such as king baboons and Goliath bird-eaters), provide a terrarium roughly a foot (30.5 cm) long on each side, and at most a foot high. Many common tarantulas will do well in a smaller container, but it is difficult to provide a water dish as well as a cover for the retreat in such a tight space.

At one time, tarantulas commonly were kept in 1-gallon (3.8 liters) screw-top jars with a few holes punched in the top for air movement. When given about 2 to 4 inches (5 to 10 cm) of substrate, the spiders did well and lived long lives. Today, the tendency is to use plastic "critter" boxes (the types that come with slotted plastic tops), small all-glass aquaria with tight-fitting lids, or plastic or glass cages custom-made to house tarantulas. You probably soon will want to expand

Shown here is a simple cage—perfect for just about any common terrestrial tarantula. Wedged into the vermiculite substrate are a water dish and retreat made from half a plastic flowerpot.

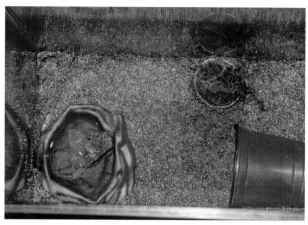

your collection beyond your first purchase, so consider using a standard size cage so several will fit evenly on a shelf, saving space and making care easier.

Tarantulas climb very well and will go up smooth glass and plastic surfaces, so the lid must fit tightly and be anchored firmly enough to keep the tarantula from forcing it open. Just putting a sheet of glass on top with a brick for weight probably won't work, as the spider will gradually shift the glass. Try to avoid very fine mesh (less than 1/4 inch [6.4 millimeters]) for the lid, as a tarantula can catch a fang in it and suffer a break; it may take several molts for the fang to regenerate. The entire top of the terrarium should either be made of screen or slotted to allow good air movement. If you need to increase humidity in the cage, place a sheet of flexible plastic (like that used to insulate windows) between the lid and the frame of the cage. By increasing or decreasing coverage of the top by the plastic, you should be able to control the humidity fairly well. Though many books recommend mesh inserts at the top and bottom of facing sides of the cage to increase air circulation, I don't feel this is necessary or practical—glass and plastic are hard to cut, mesh is hard to safely fix to the glass or plastic, and the tarantula can catch a fang in fine mesh. Side mesh panels also cause rapid loss of humidity from the cage.

It often is recommended that burrowing tarantulas be kept in shallow terraria (just a bit higher than the highest point they can reach when standing upright) to prevent

Even a terrestrial tarantula, such as this Oklahoma brown, may venture up the sides of its enclosure. A fall onto a cage accessory (or even onto the substrate from too great a height) could result in a broken appendage or even death.

injuries or death due to falls from heights greater than a foot (30.5 cm). Accidents have indeed happened in taller terraria, but generally they are not dangerous; the exception is for heavy tarantulas, whose weight increases the likelihood of injuries or death from falls.

Substrate

Though many substrates have been tried (small, round pebbles; sand; potting soil; peat moss; and sphagnum moss), the best without doubt is vermiculite. This is an inert mineral product made by heating the mineral mica, and it is widely used in horticulture. The main advantages of vermiculite are that it absorbs a great deal of water and slowly releases it; it resists fungus; and when it dries, it does not cake into a bricklike consistency (as potting soil does) or turn into dust (as peat moss does). It also is cheap and easy to find. Buy only horticultural vermiculite and make sure the label specifies that no fertilizer has been added; vermiculite used in building insulation has been treated to prevent it from absorbing water. Note that perlite is not the same as vermiculite and is not recommended. (Perlite tends to absorb less water and holds it poorly; it also sometimes sticks to an animal and can block the mouth.)

You can mix the vermiculite and water in a separate container if you wish, but when you start to construct the terrarium, it is easier to just pour in about 2 inches (5 cm) of dry vermiculite and then add clean water while mixing the two. At some point you produce a substrate that is damp to the hand but does not release water when you squeeze it. This is what you want. If you have added too much water (too wet), you can add some vermiculite to counter it; if you have too much vermiculite (too dry), add a bit more water. You can easily go to 3 or even 4 inches (7.5 to 10 cm) of substrate and not bother the tarantula.

For dedicated burrowers, vermiculite by itself often is not satisfactory, as the walls of a burrow will collapse. In such cases, it is best to use a mixture of about half potting soil and half vermiculite to give a firm burrowing substrate. Some species do better with more soil and less vermiculite,

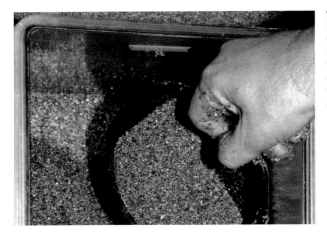

Mix your vermiculite substrate with water until it is just moist to the touch and does not seep water when you squeeze a handful.

but be aware that potting soil can dry and become solid or dusty, either of which is not good for you or the tarantula. Any mix should have at least a quarter vermiculite.

If you wish, you can add a cup of sphagnum moss to the cage to ensure that there is a relatively wet spot in the cage for emergencies (which should not happen) or put some smooth aquarium gravel or pebbles in one area to reduce the humidity. Stay away from dirt from the garden; it dries to dust and often is contaminated with fertilizers and pesticides.

Retreat Cover
If given a half flowerpot of appropriate size for the enclosure (plastic works fine and is easier to cut than pottery) wedged into the substrate in a corner, the tarantula usually will be happy to use this as the foundation of its retreat. Don't be surprised if the tarantula does not burrow in the terrarium. If the relative humidity and temperature are correct, the tarantula should be quite unstressed either staying at the surface or digging just a shallow cavity to hold its body under the flowerpot. If you don't have a flowerpot, you can use a piece of curved cork bark (very natural), a ceramic hide box made for a lizard or snake (sold widely in pet shops), or even just a clean plastic sandwich box or something similar. As long as the retreat cover gives the spider some darkness and a place to anchor its webbing, it will adapt.

Water Bowl

You can provide moisture to your spider either by misting the cage walls and retreat cover each day with room-temperature water (which will be sipped by many tarantulas) or by providing a shallow water bowl from which the spider can drink. The best solution is to give a bowl and also mist the terrarium (but not the spider) every two or three days. The bowl should be shallow enough for the spider to be able to reach the water with its mouth yet not face drowning if it falls in, but wide enough so the tarantula can maneuver the front of its body over the bowl. A standard measurement is about an inch (2.5 cm) deep and 4 inches (10 cm) wide. Shape makes no difference. Place some pebbles or rocks in the container to give crickets a way to escape when they go for a swim—crickets are fatally attracted to open water. Change the water at least every two days.

Accessories

Your tarantula needs nothing else to be comfortable. If you give it plants, it will dig them up (plus plants need special lighting, which may make it hard to keep the cage temperature down). Cute little cottages and dragons in ceramic caves will be covered with webbing and serve as inaccessible homes for vagrant crickets. The more you place in the cage, the harder it is to keep clean and sanitary. Keep things simple.

Since many tarantulas tend to climb the corners of a terrarium and then drop to the bottom when they get tired, keep hard objects out of the bottom corners of the cage. Each corner should be coated with soft substrate. If you use a heavy pottery retreat cover, place it at the center of one side of the cage, not in the corner.

Housing Tree-Dwellers

Some tropical tarantulas have made the move from the ground to shrubs and trees. There they spin thick, unsightly webs over tree holes in which they spend the day. The webbing helps them maintain the proper relative humidity and temperature for life. Consider the problems of living in a tree: wind drives down the humidity, sunlight bakes you, and a tree hole can never provide as much insulation as a burrow in the ground can. Yet tarantulas from both the New World (*Avicularia* spp. and *Psalmopoeus* spp.) and Old World (*Stromatopelma* spp. and *Poecilotheria* spp.) have made the transition successfully.

Not surprisingly, perhaps, most tree-dwelling tarantulas live quite well in a normal vermiculite-based terrarium. They tend to spend most of their time near the top and cover the sides with so much webbing that owners seldom see them, but they will feed and even breed in these circumstances. Advanced keepers, however, want to give their tree-dwellers a more natural-looking setup, so they tend to use high, narrow cages (often just 6 inches [15.2 cm] square at the base and 12 to 16 inches [30.5 to 40.6 cm] high) that contain a real or artificial branch, often with a small retreat hole, on which the spiders can attach their webbing. Many hobbyists specializing in tree-dwellers like to build their own cages of glass and plastic, but some find that turning a 20-gallon (75.6-L) aquarium on its side and building a secure cover for the now-vertical front works well for larger species. Some even house young tree-dwellers in the plastic boxes designed to hold Beanie Babies and similar stuffed toys—these boxes are roughly 4 inches square (10 cm square) and about 8 inches (20 cm) long. The cage for a tree-dweller, regardless of species, usually includes a layer of damp vermiculite in its base to supply needed humidity (in addition to daily misting). Tree-dwellers are adapted to live at a somewhat lower relative humidity level than terrestrial tarantulas are, and most will tolerate 50 percent humidity within their web retreats. Remember that humidity is measured within the retreat, not at the center of the cage. Though some can withstand quite warm temperatures and bright lights, most tarantulas are best kept in low light levels and at normal room temperatures, much as you would keep a red-knee or king baboon. These species may be tough, but they still are tarantulas.

Your arboreal species, such as the *Avicularia* sp. shown here, will appreciate a branch or piece of bark on which to hang their webs. Unlike terrestrial species that burrow into the substrate, tree-dwellers take refuge in their webs.

Make sure the branch used as the center point of the terrarium is clean. Many branches you just pick up in the yard contain ant colonies that can devastate a tarantula colony. *Colony*: that reminds me of one other difference between tree-dwellers and terrestrials. Some tree-dwellers live quite well together as long as they are of similar size, are well fed, and have a multitude of suitable retreats present so there is no fighting. There still is a risk of losing a molting tree-dwelling tarantula to its cagemate, but the risk is not as great as with terrestrials. Consider colony arrangements, but also consider the risks.

Advanced Terraria

Some terrarium hobbyists get carried away with their pets and declare that a tarantula must be in a natural-looking cage to be "happy." This obviously is not so, as a tarantula can see objects only a few inches away, needs to feel the vibrations of its prey, and will live a longer life if it never comes into contact with another tarantula. It has no admiration for plants, live or plastic, and doesn't care about decorations of any type. If the terrarium meets its basic needs, it lives a long, unstressed life.

However, you can make more elaborate cages for tarantulas if you wish. Some keepers like to be able to view their pet while it is in its burrow, so they try different methods of forcing the spider to burrow into a corner of the cage where it can be seen through the glass. A standard method is to use a block of dense florist's foam (not the air-filled Styrofoam blocks) to tightly section off a fourth to half of the terrarium; the rest of the terrarium will contain the usual vermiculite. Using a small saw or your fingers, punch a hole about an inch (2.5 cm) wide from the top of the block through the bottom. There, cut a deep quarter sphere on one side, about the length of the tarantula. When the block is wedged into place, the tarantula can enter the hole in top, travel down the tunnel to its burrow, and rest in the cavity at the base (a moist vermiculite base), where it can be seen from outside. Place a piece of dark paper over the glass to keep the spider in the dark when it isn't being observed. Use a hot soldering iron or even a heated spatula to fuse the open, cut surfaces of the foam block into a smooth finish to deter the tarantula from digging its own tunnels in the wrong directions.

Given the miracle of relatively cool fluorescent lights that produce good growth in some plants, you can try to grow simple plants such as pothos and dwarf figs in a tarantula terrarium. Place the plants in small, separate pots with the appropriate growing medium (heavy rocks around the base of the plant may keep a tarantula from digging up the plant, but may not, so avoid fertilizers) and bury them up to their rims in the substrate. Place lights well above the terrarium, and have an accurate thermometer working at all times to prevent overheating. Few plants survive well in these circumstances, so you will find yourself exchanging pots on a regular basis.

Using plastic or silk plants might work if you want to give the terrarium a more natural look. Some high-quality artificials are available, and they look good until the spider covers them with webbing and crickets start hiding in the "leaves." Plants of any type make it more difficult to keep a tarantula terrarium clean, which makes it harder for a tarantula to live an unstressed life.

Maintenance

Keeping a tarantula terrarium clean is easy, as maintenance consists mostly of spot cleaning small bits of dry tarantula feces (use a plastic spoon) and removing the carcasses of prey animals. When the webbing gets too heavy on the walls of the terrarium (which often happens with tree-dwellers and species that tend to wander rather than burrow), just scrape it off and watch the spider start over that night.

Tarantulas can move very quickly and unexpectedly, so it is always best to either remove the spider from the terrarium while cleaning or block it into its retreat with a heavy piece of wood or ceramic during the process. If you turn your back for a second while the top is not securely in place, you probably will find yourself trying to find and recapture your pet. In a deep cage, you might find that long forceps are useful for a fast spot cleaning each day.

Keep a close eye on the temperature and humidity of the cage and the retreat. When the relative humidity drops below 60 percent, add fresh water in a corner or two of the terrarium to remoisten the substrate. If you have trouble keeping the right humidity in the retreat (as may happen in air conditioned rooms, where the humidity may drop well below 50 percent), add some damp sphagnum moss (the whole plants, not processed peat moss) to the retreat.

Basic Foods

One advantage of a tarantula as a pet is that it is so easy to feed. All tarantulas feed on living animal foods, generally insects and other invertebrates that wander too close to the burrow opening at night and touch the "trap" line of silk. When the line is vibrated, the spider decodes the characters of the vibration as either food or a predator. If food, it waits until the insect comes close enough for a fast jump to allow it to grab the prey, inject it with venom, and then (usually) cover it with silk and start external digestion. If the spider finds a cricket while moving around the cage at night and the cricket freezes, the tarantula may not even recognize it as food. As a rule, if you place dead crickets in the terrarium, the tarantula will ignore them.

The normal food of pet tarantulas is the domestic or brown cricket (*Acheta domesticus*). This insect is raised by the millions (perhaps billions) on cricket farms across the

A tarantula devours its prey. The spider's external digestive juices allow it to consume the prey's liquefied insides.

country and is sold in most pet shops, through the mail, and over the Internet. Crickets are cheap and are a good food for tarantulas. Remember that the roughage of an insect is not the problem it might be when feeding it to a reptile: the spider eats only the liquefied soft tissues.

Crickets should be well fed themselves before being offered to a tarantula. You can use commercial cricket foods, a leaf of green lettuce, some shredded carrots, or unsweetened cereal—all are accepted. Give the crickets water in a small soda-bottle cap or in the form of small cubes of white potato or orange. Try to make sure the crickets have eaten before you feed them to the tarantula. No one seems to have any idea just what a tarantula needs for full and proper nutrition, but it certainly doesn't hurt to make sure its prey is healthy and well fed.

You can also occasionally feed mealworms (available in many sizes for almost any tarantula), waxworms, small Madagascan hissing cockroaches, and other cultured insects. Wild insects such as grasshoppers, dragonflies (with cut wings), and moths can be used as food, but you must be sure they are not carrying high levels of pesticides, herbicides, or fertilizers in their bodies and that they are not contaminated by heavy metals found near highways. Large beetles are generally avoided as food, as are wasps and ants of any type. Flies probably are contaminated, as are household

roaches, but cultured flightless houseflies (sometimes sold as bungee bugs) and roaches are excellent foods.

Tarantulas eat other foods such as millipedes and centipedes (obviously the largest ones can be dangerous because of their toxins and their bites, respectively), scorpions (though they may be risky from several aspects), small mice (which make a bloody mess and are not recommended), and—if waved in front of them to simulate life—small "snake sausages" made from minced mouse meat and even bits of minced liver. Live foods are essential to an unstressed tarantula, but some keepers like to push the envelope a bit and try to adapt their pets to taking dead foods. Frankly, it seems best to me to stick to crickets, which will provide a tarantula with all its nutritional needs at little risk.

Feed a wild-collected tarantula as many crickets as it will eat for the first week or two and then taper off to just a few crickets as its body fills. Most keepers try to feed their pet two or three crickets a week once they are fully acclimated and eating regularly. Remove uneaten crickets within a day after they are offered. Crickets may decide to attack a sleeping tarantula, treating it as food and they could damage a small tarantula. Some hobbyists place a small dish of cricket food in the cage to avoid this risk. Crickets often will drown in an open water bowl, so make sure they have a way of walking out of the bowl.

Don't feed insects that are too large for the tarantula. This is especially true for small and young tarantulas: the food should not be much longer than the spider's body is wide. Large prey may cause the spider to work too hard to get its food, spending more energy in the battle than it gets from digesting the insect. This may be especially true with larger grasshoppers, giant mealworms, and such strange items as pinky mice. Even the largest tarantulas do quite well on many small insects at a feeding, so just watch your spider and adjust the size and number of prey to its feeding habits.

Tarantulas often go on short fasts (or up to several months for burrowers from temperate climates), especially a few weeks before molting or laying their eggs. These fasts seldom are harmful unless the spider fails to feed for more than three or four months. A fasting tarantula may or may not break its own fast. If the keeping conditions are already satisfactory, there is little you can do to make your spider eat.

CHAPTER 4

BREEDING

L et me make my position clear from the beginning: I don't recommend that you try to breed your tarantula. Tarantulas are pets and should be treated as such. Placing them at risk of death (males) by breeding is unnecessary when dealing with most of the common tarantula species. The techniques necessary to successfully produce young tarantulas (spiderlings) can be quite complicated, with many losses of spiderlings or even entire clutches before a success. It may take three or more years before a spiderling even begins to resemble its parents; until then it looks much like an ordinary household spider. There also is no place in the pet market for the hundreds of spiderlings that could be produced by just one successful breeding of a relatively obscure species with little hobby demand. If you breed your spiders, you will either have to find some way to give the young away, feed them to pet lizards or frogs, or find the space and time to set up dozens of small jars as terraria and feed and water each little spider for months.

What follows is not meant as a recipe for breeding tarantulas. Though many hobbyists have the knack and the patience needed for breeding their pets and even turning this into a moderately successful business (if the cost of labor is excluded), it is likely that most hobbyists are not really interested in breeding their pets. The following should be considered broad guidelines to help you decide whether you might want to try a breeding or two, letting you know some of the problems you might face and how other hobbyists have handled them. Dedicated breeders have developed many ways of saving time when handling young tarantulas and know many shortcuts beyond what is mentioned here. Breeding tarantulas is a very specialized topic, but this chapter will at least give you an idea of the general procedures.

Sexing Tarantulas

Obviously, before you can breed your tarantulas, you need to have a male and a female. Getting a pair together can be tough with most tarantulas for several reasons. One problem is that males are relatively short lived compared to females, and they tend to mature before females in the same clutch mature. This is because males require fewer molts before maturity. Thus, even if the eggs of a clutch produce half males and half females, all those males probably will die long before their sisters mature. Assuming inbreeding is harmless in tarantulas (which probably is the case, as it must happen many times in burrowers with restricted distributions in small areas of habitable land), trying to raise both sexes from one egg sac seldom works. Generally, the hobby breeder tries to start out with a mature female (either raised from a spiderling or purchased as a juvenile or an adult) and buys, rents, or borrows a mature male of the right species when the owner feels the female is ready to mate.

The other problem is that sexing tarantulas is difficult. As a rule, males are recognizable only once they go through their last molt and suddenly develop visible secondary sex organs on the pedipalps (and sometimes the first legs). Females gradually become mature, and there is no true way of determining just when a female moves from immature to mature, so a lot of guesswork is involved.

Males

Let's start with males. Males as a rule are a bit smaller than females of the same species and population, and they tend to have longer, thinner legs and a smaller, sometimes almost shrunken-looking abdomen. Occasionally, their colors and patterns are slightly different in details, and possibly the details of some areas of climbing bristles on the legs (the scopulae) may differ between sexes. When the male makes its molt to the sexually mature form—usually sometime between one and three years of age—this is the end of its growth, and the spider will not successfully molt again. With this molt, it develops fairly obvious external characters that allow it to be sexed.

A close-up look at this male orange-striped bird eater (also called a Goliath striped-leg) shows the embolus that contains the male's sperm.

First, the tarsus of each pedipalp becomes strongly modified. The segment generally becomes widened or twisted into a clawless structure called the cymbium that is scooped out underneath to hide an oval sperm bulb that ends in a hollow process called the embolus. When not in use, the sperm bulb is held in a horizontal position against the cymbium and may not be easily visible, but you should be able to detect that the segment itself is not normal and then notice the swollen bulb. In the majority of common tarantulas, the mature male also develops a large blackish hook or spine at the end of the tibia of each first walking leg. This is known as the tibial apophysis (plural, apophyses). Though sometimes partially hidden under long bristles under the legs, if you look closely, you can see the apophyses.

Additionally, in many male tarantulas, you can see a shallow, straight epigastric furrow running between the two anterior book lungs. Running from the furrow forward toward the pedicel is a pair of nearly parallel indented lines, usually with a slightly raised, whitish oval area between them. This is the ventral spinning field of the male, from which it spins some of its sperm web (discussion following).

Females

Mature females tend to be a bit larger than mature males, with thicker legs and larger abdomens. Maturity is gradual in females, and it may take three to six years for some larger tarantulas to mature. To determine the sex of a living tarantula that lacks obvious sperm bulbs, you must turn it over (carefully) and observe the base of the abdomen under magnification and good light. As in the male, the epigastric furrow runs between the two anterior book lungs, but in a mature female it is a raised, clifflike area that often is obvious in lateral view. As a rule, the higher the cliff, the more likely that the tarantula is mature. There generally is a trapezoidal area (not a square as in males) lacking a pale spot in the center in front of the epigastric furrow.

Sexing from Molted Skins

Handling a tarantula always is problematic, and holding it upside down can be stressful to both you and the spider. Instead, many breeders prefer to determine sex, especially of females, by examining cast skins under a microscope. The procedure is moderately complicated and requires both experience with a variety of species at different ages and a reference collection of shed skins, preferably of spiders followed through to their maturity molts (males) or to the laying of eggs (females). In basic terms, the skin is soaked in soapy water to make it flexible, and then the underside of the anterior abdomen is examined. Remember that you are looking at the skin from the inside out, preferably with a bright light shining through the skin toward the observer. (At least a 10x loupe is required, and a stereomicroscope is much better.) Find the four book lungs, which appear as two pairs of whitish squares. Between the generally smaller front pair will be the epigastric furrow, and in the center of this will be a pore that is the primary opening to the internal sexual organs. In a male, the furrow is simple and low, without projections. In a female, even an immature one, there should be small tubes or pockets to the front of the furrow; these are the spermathecae (singular, spermatheca), which are sacs in which the female stores sperm inserted by the male to fertilize the eggs at a later date. As a rule, the tubes are narrow, are widely separated along the furrow, and end in rounded bulbs, but they also may end in a pair of bulbs (as in king baboons) or have very wide bases that together cover much of the length of the furrow and are much wider than the bulbs at their ends (Costa Rican striped-knee). In most of the common *Brachypelma* species (including the red-knee and painted red-leg), the spermathecae are fused into a single oval pocket the width of the furrow and lack distinct external bulbs. Regardless of shape, the shed skin of a female tarantula more than about six months to a year old should show the spermathecae.

Some tarantula clubs and experts offer to sex your tarantula from a shed skin. The price is low and the degree of accuracy is high, so if the service is available, utilize it.

Reproductive Cycles

In nature, male tarantulas usually roam about after their sexual molt, looking for females. After the first mating, they may succeed in finding one or two other receptive females and mate again before slowly losing strength (often, they do not eat and do expend much energy) and dying, generally within six months to a year of the molt. The female remains in her burrow, mates there, chases off the male, and lays eggs roughly three to six months after mating. The eggs are surrounded by a silken egg case that either is carried around with the female under her body, held by the chelicerae (in most American species) or is hung within the spider's burrow (in some Old World species). Hatching takes six to eight weeks, often requiring the assistance of the mother to tear apart the case so the young can escape. Each spiderling is on its own, building its own tiny burrow.

In the terrarium, things are a bit different. Though some keepers believe that in nature different tarantulas breed at different seasons, in captivity any such tendencies soon are lost, as captive-bred tarantulas breed almost any time of the year. When a male molts to the sexual form (generally you will notice the sperm bulb), he should be given about two months to assure that he has developed active sperm before considering mating him. A sexual male may be very nervous, constantly tries to escape (especially if he can smell hormones from a female in the same room), and often does not eat. Females, on the other hand, tend to remain placid even when they are fully mature and receptive, and they seldom wander to look for a male (or for any other reason).

In the United States, male *Aphonopelma* spp. tarantulas often are found wandering roads looking for female burrows in later summer or early autumn. It often is assumed that they mate then and die during the following winter, but recent studies in Arkansas that show some males may survive the winter and still be fully active the following spring, though they are virtually absent during the early summer. This probably means that in nature these males molted into adult form in perhaps July and died in May, living about ten or eleven months. In captivity, immature males that are not fed heavily may mature slower than those fed freely, which means that you can slow the rate of maturity a bit if desired. Keeping adult males relatively cool and away from the smells of females may allow them to live a bit longer, especially if they can be made to eat.

A mature female becomes receptive after a molt, so she will have a clean skin and a clean area around the epigastric furrow and spermathecae. Typically, a breeder gives the female a month or two to fully harden and eat several rich meals before being allowed to mate.

Place the cage containing the male next to the cage containing the female. You may want to use a slightly larger cage than normal, at least 16 inches (40 cm) square, to give the male more maneuvering room during mating and help ensure his safety. Within hours of noticing the female, the male will start a courtship dance, thumping on the floor with his feet and pedipalps. That night he will build a small web (sperm web) in his cage and crawl under it upside down, so his abdominal genital pore (between the front book lungs) lies against the web. He releases a few drops of sperm onto the web, then climbs over the web so his pedipalps are over the drops of sperm. Wetting the tips of the emboli (the projections from the sperm bulbs) a bit in the mouth, he then uses capillary action from the bulb to pull some sperm into each bulb through the emboli. The sperm is stored in a short, coiled tube in the bulb. He's now ready to mate. After one use, the sperm web is torn down, so you may not notice this entire procedure.

Now it is time to place the tarantulas together. Be careful and watch the behavior of the spiders. If the female is not ready to mate (not receptive), she will rush the male and may try to kill him as she would any other strange tarantula. You may have to separate the two with a piece of cardboard and a foot-long (30.5 cm) length of slender dowel, and remove the male to try again a week or so later.

The male continues his thumping courtship dance in the presence of the female and can read her mood, judging whether he can approach her. If all is well, he moves closer and runs his pedipalps and front legs over her in a calming caress, and the female backs up and raises her body so the front legs are off the ground and her abdominal genital pore is accessible.

For many tarantulas, mating is relatively peaceful, but for some it is dangerous for the male. As a rule, few males are killed during mating. To gain an advantage, the male uses the apophyses, or hooks on the first legs (if he has apophyses—not all species do), to lock the female's fangs in place; then he lifts her body with his front legs. At this point, he inserts one or both emboli into her genital pore, transferring thousands of sperm cells in one or two droplets. These quickly migrate into the spermathecae, where they can survive for months. Copulation takes only seconds, and then the male unhooks, lets the female down, and heads for another part of the terrarium. Sometimes the female will chase him and try to kill (and eat) him, but more often she just ignores him and returns to her burrow.

Remove the male to his terrarium, give him a couple of weeks to recover, try to get him to feed, and he will be ready for another mating with the same or a different female. Some keepers have been able to keep males of a few Old World and tree-dwelling tarantulas (especially *Avicularia* species) together with their mates for weeks, but this really is dangerous and could be deadly.

Caring for Egg Cases

For the next three to six months, the female continues life as usual, though she should be fed more heavily if possible to help her build up food reserves before laying. Eventually she

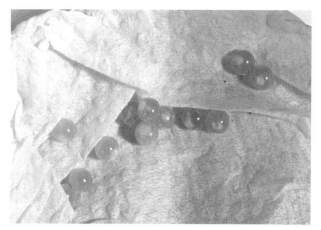

Each of these Peruvian pink-toe eggs is about 5 millimeters in diameter.

will construct a loose web in her burrow and either molt or lay eggs. If she molts, the sperm are cast aside with her old exoskeleton, and she can no longer lay fertile eggs. If instead she comes out without molting and rolls the web into a stiff (usually oval) case then she has laid her eggs. Tarantulas may lay from less than a hundred (*Theraphosa* spp.) to more than a thousand (*Citharischius* spp.) eggs in a clutch, with no obvious correlation between clutch size and age of the female.

Normally, females guard their egg cases by hovering over them, protecting them from attacks by ants, other spiders, predatory insects, and possibly fungus. If stressed, the female may rip open the case and eat her eggs (which admittedly are a good food but certainly not the result you are looking for), so, leave her alone as much as possible. A guarding female usually continues to eat (some keepers withhold food to prevent insects disturbing the case) and otherwise behaves fairly normally. If the egg case is hung in a dense web placed within the burrow and not pro-tected under the body of the mother, the female may become even more aggressive than normal. Each day the mother rotates the egg case several times, equivalent to a hen turning her eggs.

If you leave the egg case with the female, you will notice after about six weeks that the case has been torn apart and the eggs are missing. If you look carefully, you should notice at least some spiderlings in tiny burrows scattered over the cage bottom, where they probably will die because you will not be able to feed them or even separate them from the mother. For this reason, most breeders corner the female after she has cared for the case for a month and remove the egg case to a separate container, where it can be watched and the young rescued immediately. Remember that mother tarantulas may be exceptionally aggressive.

Generally the egg case is placed in a small plastic cup (such as a cup used for delicatessen salads) with a cover to keep the humidity at 65 percent. Roll the case at least three or four times a day. In about two weeks, the eggs should be six weeks old and, for most species, near hatching. Carefully slit the case open with small scissors and pour the contents into a shallow covered dish (such as a petri dish) with a circle of laboratory filter paper on the bottom. The eggs may be in any of three or four stages of development. Some will be simply round cream to brown eggs that are still far from hatching. Others (perhaps the great majority) will be postembryos, which look like an unmoving hump holding on to the egg with partially developed legs. The postembryo cannot move and is still using the yolk of the egg to continue development. If kept clean and at about 65 percent humidity, these will continue to develop into spiderlings.

In many cases, most of what is released from the egg case will be first instars, which look like pale, often transparent, little spiders that can move around and feed. These generally molt within a few days into second instars, which have more substance and often the beginnings of a color pattern (which seldom comes close to that of the adult). At this point, the yolk sac has been absorbed and the spiderlings are distinct little individuals.

Caring for Spiderlings

The care of spiderlings requires multitudes of small containers, usually glass or plastic vials or baby-food jars of about the same size for ease of handling. Fill each jar halfway with moist (but not wet) vermiculite, or with a mix of sterilized potting soil and moist vermiculite. The lid

Mombasa golden starbursts, such as these spiderlings, are probably the only African tarantulas docile enough for beginning hobbyists, as most species from the continent are quite aggressive.

is punched with a few pinholes or closed with a wad of sterile cotton or foam to allow some air circulation while letting the substrate remain moist. Each container can house only one spiderling, so if the egg case holds three hundred eggs that develop fully into spiderlings, you will need three hundred containers plus the shelf space to house them securely. Often groups of containers are placed in larger plastic boxes to help control the humidity, which should run about 65 percent to 70 percent for most species.

As soon as a spiderling is placed in a container, it will make its first little burrow and expect food to wander by. Most spiderlings will take a pinhead cricket (the size just after hatching, before more than one or two molts) or a micro mealworm (usually the larvae of small flour beetles), but very small spiderlings may need flightless fruit flies (*Drosophila* spp.). The size of the food must match the size of the spiderling and, of course, will have to change as the spider grows. Often spiderlings will attack the dead body or at least the abdomen of a freshly killed cricket if it is split open so juices are easier to get to.

Most spiderlings are fed three to four times a week at first, and their containers have to be cleaned of waste and dried insect husks a day after each feeding. Check the substrate at cleaning time to make sure it has not dried out too much. This means that every week you will be opening

This juvenile Antillean (also called the Martinique tarantula for its natural habitat on Martinique in the Caribbean) pink-toe's bold blue color will fade with each molt. As hinted in its scientific name, *Avicularia versicolor*, its colors change as the spider grows to pinks and reds with a stunning metallic blue-green carapace.

and closing each container three or four times (assuming you wait until the next feeding to clean the cage). Multiply this times three hundred containers each time, and you can start to imagine how much patience and time you need to raise spiderlings.

As the spiderlings grow (some individuals grow faster than others, even on the same diet, and different species also grow at different rates), they will have to be moved to larger containers appropriate to their size. This is one advantage of baby-food jars, which can house a young tarantula longer than smaller vials can. On the other hand, a spiderling is easier to see in a vial (remember, they are somewhat translucent and burrowed in), and it is easier to see possible problem infestations such as mites, fly larvae, and the occasional vagrant, blood-thirsty cricket (which can eat a spiderling if allowed to grow). Have you also thought about how much three hundred baby-food jars partially filled with substrate will weigh?

With luck, each spiderling will molt about six to ten times during its first year, about half as many times in the second year, and perhaps two or three times in the third. By year three the immature tarantulas look like the parents but are smaller, often with slightly different color patterns (such as the brightly banded abdomens of *Avicularia* species) and often with different leg shapes and a less bulky body. Only a few tarantulas look much like the adults after their first year of life. They now can be transferred to the usual terraria, one per container, and treated much like adult tarantulas, allowing for their small size. The first time you try to raise tarantulas outside an egg case you probably will have many spiderling losses due to fungus: it grows in substrate that is too wet and not cleaned often enough. You may get infestations of either mites (which compete with spiderlings for food and may attack the spider as well) or tiny humpbacked phorid flies, which may lay their eggs on the spiderling and cause its death. Keeping spiderling containers balanced between the proper humidity and feeding conditions versus cleanliness is difficult and learned only by experience. Not everyone has the patience to raise spiderlings, so don't be disappointed if you don't succeed. Besides, what do you do with three hundred brownish tarantulas that won't be salable for at least three years?

A juvenile Colombian bird-eating spider feeds on a cricket. Most spiderlings require three to four feedings per week.

CHAPTER 5

HEALTH MAINTENANCE

W hen you keep your tarantula in the proper type of cage and feed it well, it is likely to live out its life without problems. This is especially true of captive-bred specimens. Most of the problems that shorten a tarantula's life are due to improper handling and a failure to keep it clean. These big spiders are among the hardiest of animals.

Accidents

Next to molt-related deaths, the worst things that can happen to a tarantula occur when it is handled—mishandled, actually. Considering the way a spider's body is constructed, a fall from any significant distance (greater than a foot [30 cm]) onto a hard or sharp surface is almost certain to rupture the abdomen. Remember that a tarantula does not have arteries and veins as humans do; instead, it has an open circulatory system that flows and oozes hemolymph at low pressure through cavities or sinuses throughout the body. Even the heart is unprotected at the top of the abdomen under a thin skin. Hemolymph accounts for about 20 percent of the weight of a tarantula. Drop a tarantula and it can rupture like a melon.

Can you do anything about a rupture? First, don't handle the spider where it might fall—this is the reason for the recommendation to always shuffle it into a glass or box to transfer it from point to point and to keep hard objects out of the corners of the relatively low terrarium. Keepers whose tarantulas have fallen and suffered relatively minor ruptures with uncontrolled oozing of hemolymph (which is a pale bluish fluid) have tried with some success to slow the flow by covering the break with a layer of toilet paper (as you would a shaving cut) and then coating this with flour or cornstarch to induce clotting. Contrary to statements in some books, tarantula blood contains a very efficient clotting mechanism, and small breaks will clot and heal just as they would in a vertebrate. A bleeding tarantula needs free access to drinking water; hydration will help its body almost immediately replenish lost blood.

Another common accident is loss of a leg or other appendage. This can happen during fights, by getting a leg stuck in a tight spot, or by breaking off the tip of a fang in fine mesh or on hard prey. Eventually, most broken appendages will regenerate to at least a semblance of the original member, but it may take several molts, which means that an older adult (which seldom molts) will never complete the process. The worst case scenario is when the break occurs between the joints of a leg or pedipalp, where bleeding is virtually uncontrolled. The limbs are supplied with much blood because the blood helps increase hydraulic pressure within a limb, producing movement. There are special valves at the joints of the limbs that can close to restrict blood flow below them; so, if the break occurs at a joint, bleeding will be limited. What usually happens with a broken limb is that the spider uses its chelicerae to twist off the broken, bleeding segment below the closest valve. It may lose the leg, but at least bleeding is stopped, and when you normally have eight legs, having only seven is not a great disadvantage. When a break occurs during molting, you may have to go in and twist off the broken segment because the weak, soft tarantula may be unable to do it. Just move quickly and deliberately; sharply twist off the bleeding leg at the top of the segment to activate the valve.

Parasites and Pests

Like other animals, tarantulas carry an abundance of intestinal worms and other parasites that are part of their normal gut fauna and probably don't harm them under unstressful conditions. Even captive-bred tarantulas undoubtedly have a good number of parasites that were passed to them by the parent through the egg. We can't control these pests, so there is no real reason to worry about them.

Occasionally you will find small, dark mites (with eight or sometimes six legs and flattened, oval to round bodies) crawling on a tarantula. These usually are mites that simply are carried about by the tarantula and share the leftover food near the mouthparts. They are harmless, but many people find them annoying. You can pick them off individually by dipping a blunt toothpick in petroleum jelly and "spearing" each one, but this is hardly efficient. Miticides sold in pet shops may kill tarantulas and shouldn't be used.

More dangerous are tiny translucent mites that live in the substrate and feed on old food and wastes. These are said to attack tarantulas and feed on their body fluids, though I've seen little to support this. The best remedy is to completely clean the cage or move the tarantulas to new cages after inspecting the spiders in a bright light (watch the heat from the light, which could cause dehydration) and removing any mites.

Phorid flies are tiny humpbacked flies that feed on wastes and can become a nuisance in a spiderling-rearing jar. Their larvae are said to actually feed on tiny tarantulas if all other foods disappear. Keep the cage clean and transfer the spider to a new cage if you see an infestation. These flies are smaller than fruit flies, are usually brown in color, and have a distinctive humped shape when viewed with a magnification lens.

In some books, much is made of tarantula hawks or hunters (actually called pepsids by entomologists and are members of the spider-wasp family, Pompilidae) that attack tarantulas in the wild. A spider-wasp stings a tarantula with a paralyzing toxin and lays an egg on the spider. Then she hauls the tarantula into a shallow hole that she's dug. The developing larva eats its way through the living tarantula, killing it when the larva leaves to pupate in the ground before turning into the adult wasp. These big (up to 2 inches [5 cm]) smoky-winged iridescent wasps are common in the southwestern areas of the United States, but I doubt that they could ever invade your tarantula room. Other insects (especially certain groups of flies) may have larvae that develop within living tarantulas as well. Occasionally, a wild-caught tarantula will harbor a larva of one of these flies, leading to its eventual death.

Almost certainly your tarantula room will at some time be invaded by ants, which can find their way into any building. If you get a heavy enough invasion, ants can find and kill any tarantula by biting, stinging, and chewing it to death. Ant baits in enclosed plastic tabs can be scattered around the floor of the room for good control. An even simpler method is to put a dish of water under each leg of the table that supports the tarantula cages, if possible; ants won't be able to move over the water to the leg, as least in most cases. Never use ant sprays or dusts near tarantulas; these will kill most invertebrates.

Molting

Many hobbyists fear the molt because of the possibility of a molt-related death. However, this separation of the new and old exoskeletons is essential if the tarantula is to grow. The new skin is fully developed under the old skin up to several weeks before the molt; the old skin must shed to allow the new skin to be exposed, fill with fluids, and harden upon contact with the air. A healthy tarantula should have no trouble during a molt, except possibly a broken leg, and it usually can take care of this itself. Death occasionally occurs for unknown reasons, perhaps due to an internal problem in the tarantula that we cannot detect, but since an adult tarantula probably has gone through more than a dozen molts, the process must be quite safe.

This Chilean rose tarantula is finishing a molt.

Many tarantulas turn on their backs to molt, possibly because they find it easier to pull their legs out of the old skin downward rather than upward. In American tarantulas that have rubbed the top of the abdomen bare, you sometimes can notice a darkening of the area caused by hemolymph accumulating between the old and new skins, but otherwise the only sign of impending molting may be that the spider stops feeding for a week or two. Molting generally takes place at night, in a secluded corner or under a cover, and may take just an hour or less. The old skin splits at the front and side edges of the carapace, and the tarantula simply pulls its entire body out through the opening. All chitinous surfaces are molted, which includes not only the mouthparts, but also the lining of the gut and other internal structures. The cast skin is a nearly perfect reproduction of the tarantula, as you might expect, and is helpful for sexing young tarantulas and correctly identifying species. Shed skins commonly are taken out, dried, wrapped loosely in tissue paper, and stored in labeled boxes for a record of growth.

In theory, the environment should have little to do with the success of a molt, but observations indicate that a tarantula that is kept too dry will have more chances of dying during a molt. Perhaps if the relative humidity is too low (less than 60 percent) the odds increase that the new skin will dry to inflexibility before it can be pulled out of the old skin. Regardless, help prevent problems by making sure the humidity near the molting tarantula is sufficient.

Environmental Problems

If kept improperly, a tarantula will be unhealthy, not feed, be highly stressed, and die. You must be sure that the temperature of the terrarium is correct (generally 70°F to 85°F [21°C to 29.4°C] is the best range) and the relative humidity is between 60 and 70 percent. Prevent problems with bacteria, parasites, and pests by keeping the cage clean; do not allow waste to accumulate in the corners of the cage. Crickets can carry mites, fungi, and bacteria into the cage, all of which will grow in waste and later cause problems.

Avoid direct sunlight on tarantulas—they are nocturnal, remember, and even the tree-dwellers have trouble maintaining proper temperature and humidity in sunlight. Be careful that any lightbulbs or heaters are not too warm and are never accessible to the tarantula. Webbing of virtually any surface of the terrarium is not considered a problem (it is natural with many species), but you can remove it by just pulling and scraping it off; the spider will quickly replace it, however.

Keep the substrate properly moist. All substrates dry over time, so the water should be replenished periodically (usually by pouring small amounts into the corners until the consistency is correct). Be aware that any substrate based on peat moss will dry into a dangerous dust, and any based on dirt may dry into a bricklike consistency that is useless for a tarantula. Stick to vermiculite if at all possible.

If you keep these simple precautions in mind, your tarantula should live through its six to twenty years of adult life with few problems (only female tarantulas typically live beyond six years; males have short lives regardless of conditions). Tarantulas have not survived four hundred million years by being delicate.

A Chilean rose tarantula rests on a branch.

CHAPTER 6

NOTES ON SELECTED TARANTULAS

Scientists recognize more than eight hundred species of true tarantulas (family Theraphosidae) with perhaps a few hundred still to be described. A surprisingly large percentage of these recognized species, perhaps 10 percent, are available to hobbyists, though many are either difficult to keep or quite expensive and thus not likely to be a good choice for beginning and intermediate hobbyists.

Introduction to Identification

One of the first things a hobbyist is likely to notice is that the identifications of tarantulas, even of the common species, are uncertain, with dealers and scientists often applying different names to what seems to be a single species or type (one of its subspecies or varieties). One reason for this uncertainty is that much of the older literature naming tarantulas is incomplete and often inaccurate, and type specimens were not always saved, so scientists today cannot look at them for new information useful in identifications. Many scientists who described tarantulas a hundred or even fifty years ago did so without considering variation within a species—or the possibility that a single species might have a wide range and show only small differences in proportions or color over this range. Additionally, there have been different philosophies of taxonomy (the identification and naming of species and other groups) in use over the years, and one person's species may be another's genus or subspecies. Regardless, scientific names of tarantulas change often and can be confusing. Common names are not stable and vary from country to country and from year to year, as well as from author to author. No one has come up with a full catalog of all the valid species of tarantulas, with stable scientific names and usable common names in any language.

Features of Importance

Identifying tarantulas is seldom straightforward; however, as the common species become more readily available as captive-bred specimens, there is less variation to be expected in a single species. Look first at the general appearance of the spider. Is it exceptionally hairy or smooth? Is one pair of legs much longer or heavier than the others? Is there a horn or tubercle on the carapace? Is there an obvious color pattern on the carapace or abdomen? For that matter, is there a strong color pattern on the legs, and if so which segments of the leg have the color? Is the red ring on the patella (knee) or on the top of the tibia? Though many tarantulas are shades of brown and black, a surprising number of the most commonly kept species have distinctive and constant color patterns that are easy to learn and remember.

To a specialist, most of the features mentioned above are just secondary. What counts are details of structure. Are there thick-based bristles at the sides of the chelicerae, pedipalps, or first walking legs? For that matter, are there long or strongly modified bristles on any part of the body? Are there teeth on the chelicerae other than the fangs? Is the foveal groove straight or curved? Are there secondary grooves on the cephalothorax? If you look closely (with a microscope or strong magnifying loupe), are there special pads of bristles (scopulae) under the first two segments of the legs that help the tarantula climb? What is the detailed structure of the sperm bulb and its point (embolus), as well as the projecting part of the tarsus above it? In a female, what is the structure of spermathecae extending from the epigastric furrow that are used to store sperm?

It also is important to know where a tarantula originally came from. A surprising number of unrelated tarantulas from the Americas and Asia, for instance, look much alike at first and even second glance. Sometimes even behavior can be a useful feature: American tarantulas often have nearly bare upper abdomens because they have scraped off the urticating bristles; African and Asian tarantulas lack these bristles and thus shouldn't have a bare patch on the abdomen.

Names

All tarantulas that have been described by scientists carry scientific names, which are written in italics to set them off from surrounding text. These names all are based on Latin, Greek, or at least Latinized words from other languages. A complete scientific name consists of the genus (plural, genera) written as a capitalized word (equivalent to a last or family name for humans) and a specific name—the species (*species* is both singular and plural)—that is never capitalized. The specific name is similar to your first or given name. Therefore, the name Joe Doe as a scientific name might be given as *Doeus josephus*. Often the scientific name is accompanied by the name of the scientist who described the species and the date: *Aphonopelma hentzi* (Girard 1854). When the describer's name is in parentheses, it indicates the species was originally described in a different genus—a very common case in tarantulas.

Species

What is a species? Opinions vary among scientists and hobbyists. As a general rule, a species can be a group of populations that share a similar appearance and can freely breed with one another in nature to produce fertile offspring that resemble the parents. Species have a distinct range, usually defined by geographical or ecological barriers, but two very similar species may occupy the same range when separated by behavioral or physiological differences that prevent successful interbreeding (hybridization). A subspecies is a group of populations within the range of a species that differs in some detail of features yet is capable of breeding successfully with other populations of the species. Two subspecies cannot occupy the same range, as they would continually interbreed to produce intermediate offspring that would not have the characters of the parents.

Length is measured from the tip of the chelicerae to the end of the abdomen. *Leg span* is measured from tip to tip of the longest pair of legs, lying flat; leg span is roughly three times a spider's body length.

Some American Tarantulas

As a rule, American tarantulas have less aggressive personalities than those of the Old World and are better suited for beginners. They generally tolerate more abuse and accidents, and few have a truly dangerous bite. Most do kick urticating hairs off the abdomen, however. Many species are available inexpensively as captive-bred spiderlings of decent size for you to raise to maturity in three to six years.

Oklahoma Brown
Aphonopelma hentzi (Girard 1854)

We start with a plain, brownish, shaggy tarantula representing one or perhaps several species found from Arkansas and Louisiana west to Oklahoma and probably at least through eastern Texas. The Oklahoma brown (also called Texas brown) has a 2-inch (5-cm) approximate body length and is one of several species of *Aphonopelma* that can be collected during the spring and autumn in much of the southwestern United States. (The species in genus *Aphonopelma* all look alike, are virtually impossible to identify correctly at this time, and can be kept in the same fashion. They are sold

Looking closely at this Oklahoma brown, you can see it's missing its second leg. The injury—a result from a fall onto a cage decoration—healed eventually, but the tarantula's appendage will not regenerate until many molts have occurred.

under a variety of names but basically represent one biological type.) These tarantulas enjoy relatively dry surroundings and can either burrow or be quite unstressed if given a retreat cover over vermiculite. Though not colorful (their cephalothoraxes are golden tan or pale tan, and their abdomens and legs are brown), they are easy to deal with and adapt quickly to the terrarium. Their bite is temporarily painful, however, and they move quickly and climb very efficiently. Captive breeding is uncommon because there is no market for the hundred or more young produced in an egg case.

Rio Grande Gold
Aphonopelma moderatum
(Chamberlin & Ivie 1939)

Found along the Rio Grande in southern Texas (and presumably on the Mexican side as well), this is another brown tarantula that can be collected and kept in a simple setup, though some believe it prefers a deep substrate in which to burrow. It has a 2-inch (5-cm) body length. The main feature of the species is the presence of dense, golden-tan bristles over the brown of the abdomen, carapace, and legs, giving the species a distinctive appearance. The related desert blond tarantula (*Aphonopelma chalcodes*) has dense, short, golden hairs covering the cephalothorax and reddish bristles on the abdomen; it is from southern Arizona. Both species are uncommonly collected and rarely bred in numbers.

One way you can distinguish this Rio Grande gold tarantula from a similar-looking desert blond tarantula is by inspecting its abdominal bristles. The Rio Grande's urticating hairs are golden, whereas the desert's bristles are generally red.

Costa Rican Striped-Knee (Zebra)
Aphonopelma seemanni
(F. P.-Cambridge 1897)

This species from tropical forests of Costa Rica is one of the most popular and widely available tarantulas in the United States. Females and some males have a distinctive pattern of paired white stripes on the knee (patella) and tibia of each leg plus a narrow, white front edge of the cephalothorax. It has a 2.5-inch (6.3-cm) body length. It needs a quite humid terrarium (preferably 70 percent) and room to burrow into a firm substrate of vermiculite with potting soil. Make sure there is a large water dish. Though popular, striped-knees also have a reputation for being nervous tarantulas that sometimes bite. Because most still are imported, they are not always in the best of health when found.

The Costa Rican striped-knee tarantula is nicknamed zebra because of the black and white striping on its legs.

Common Pink-Toe
Avicularia avicularia (Linnaeus 1758)

Perhaps the most commonly sold tree-dwelling tarantula, the common pink-toe is found in open forests over much of northern South America and is available both as imports and captive-bred specimens. Adults are shaggy, black tarantulas with bright to dull pinkish pads of hairs at the ends of the legs and a 2-inch (5-cm) body length. Young specimens may be more brightly colored than older adults and still show some blue banding on the abdomen. This

The common pink-toe tarantula can be hard to distinguish from other pink-toed species such as the Antillean shown below. Your best clue is to look for a mostly black body with pink hairs only on the ends of the legs like this specimen.

species does best in a tall terrarium with only a bit of substrate and a group of branches on which to build thick web retreats. These are fast spiders that can jump long distances, and they can be hard to handle. It is possible to keep more than one in a very large terrarium with heavy feedings, but cannibalism probably will occur. Several similar species are imported and are hard to distinguish. The common pink-toe was one of the first tarantulas described by Western science.

Antillean Pink-Toe
Avicularia versicolor (Walckenaer 1837)

This tree-dwelling species comes from the islands of Martinique and Guadeloupe in the southern Caribbean

Still a juvenile, this Antillean pink-toe tarantula retains a bluish abdomen. As its scientific name, *Avicularia versicolor*, suggests, the spider's colors change as it grows to adulthood. The abdomen usually turns from blue to pink or red and the carapace develops a metallic green hue.

and is considered one of the most colorful tarantulas available today. Adult male Antilleans are shaggy spiders with small but distinctly pink to white toe tips and reddish brown bristles on the legs. The abdomen is clothed in bright red bristles, while the smooth cephalothorax may be brilliant metallic green with blue reflections. As the spider grows, it will lose its bright blue hue; as an adult its colors turn from blue to pink and red with a metallic green carapace. Though captive-bred, it remains expensive. It has a 2-inch (5-cm) body length.

Curly-Hair
Brachypelma albopilosum (Valerio 1980)
Another species often imported from humid forests of Costa Rica and adjacent countries, the blackish brown curly-hair tarantula likes a humid terrarium (preferably at least 70 to as much as 80 percent relative humidity). The curly-hair tarantula needs a deep substrate for burrowing, though it survives well if given just a retreat cover such as an overturned partial flowerpot. Far from colorful, its main claim to fame is that the abdomen is covered with long tan to white hairs that are distinctively curved or curled at the ends. Similar hairs occur on the legs. If you can find captive-bred specimens (which are healthier and more adaptable than imports), this makes an excellent beginner's tarantula as it is not especially aggressive. It has a 2-inch (5-cm) body length.

On this curly-hair tarantula, you can see the trademark long, tan abdominal hairs.

Painted (Mexican) Red-Leg
Brachypelma emilia (White 1856)

One of the most familiar and beautiful of the tarantulas, this species is widely available as captive-bred specimens, as importation from Mexico has been illegal for two decades. It has a 2-inch (5-cm) body length, and the tibia of the legs are reddish brown and covered with long reddish bristles, with black segments above and below. The carapace is coppery tan with a wide, black triangle extending forward from the foveal groove. These two features together make it virtually unmistakable. Red-legs are calm, adaptable tarantulas that fit into most simple terrarium setups and are almost problem free once they are about half grown. They are highly recommended for beginners.

Mexican Red-Knee
Brachypelma smithi (F. P.-Cambridge 1897)

Protected for two decades, the Mexican red-knee is now a relatively expensive tarantula available as captive-bred spiderlings at a moderate cost or as adults at a high cost. At either age, it is easy to care for and adapts well to the terrarium. It has a 2.5-inch (6.3-cm) body length. The patella (knee) is covered with reddish orange bristles, and the segments above this are deep black, providing high contrast. The carapace is velvety black with a narrow coppery brown rim. The flame-knee tarantula (*Brachypelma auratum*) is

The orange red bristles on the patellae distinguish this Mexican red-knee tarantula from the similar looking flame-knee tarantula.

72

very similar, except the patella is dark red, without a touch of orange; the two are not always easy to distinguish. Sometimes seen is the more expensive and more spectacular flame-leg tarantula (*Brachypelma boehmei*), which has a reddish brown patella, tibia, and metatarsus, and the entire cephalothorax is bright copper. Red-legs, red-knees, and flame-legs all come from relatively dry highlands of Mexico and are protected, so only purchase captive-bred specimens. All can be kept in much the same fashion in a simple terrarium at 60 percent humidity. Some keepers have developed painful sores from the urticating hairs of these species, but others have had few problems.

Mexican Red-Rump
Brachypelma vagans (Ausserer 1875)
Another Mexican and Central American species protected by law from importation, the red-rump is a black tarantula without bright colors on the legs but with long, bright reddish brown bristles on the abdomen. It has a 2-inch (5-cm) body length. Most specimens now available are captive-bred and not inexpensive. Keep the enclosure a bit more humid than normal (perhaps to 70 percent relative humidity) and mix some potting soil into the vermiculite substrate to allow easier burrowing.

Green Bottle Blue
Chromatopelma cyaneopubescens
(Strand 1907)
This species caused a sensation when it was introduced a few years ago, and it certainly is beautiful. The carapace is bright blue with green reflections, and the abdomen is covered with red bristles. The legs, in contrast, are covered with deep blue bristles, giving the species a distinctive appearance. This Venezuelan species now is widely bred in captivity. Adults will reach a 2-inch (5-cm) body length and will do well in a simple setup at moderate humidity; young specimens are semiarboreal, building webs at the bases of tall grasses and shrubs. Young may have to be misted regularly to give them sufficient humidity.

The striking, orange red abdomen of this green bottle blue tarantula is quite a contrasting backdrop for its bold, blue legs.

Chilean Rose
Grammostola rosea (Walckenaer 1837)

One of the most commonly sold tarantulas, the Chilean rose has a 2-inch (5-cm) body length and is an overall brownish, shaggy tarantula that displays typically faint rosy reflections at the front of the carapace. Some specimens are more bronze than rosy, and some have an obviously pinkish hue. This species seems to be a wanderer that may not build permanent burrows in its home range or in the terrarium, and it does fine with just a retreat cover and moderate humidity. Unfortunately, it has proved difficult to breed in captivity, but thousands are imported from Chile and make decent, though sometimes nervous and aggressive, pets.

The faint, pinkish tint of this Chilean rose tarantula is easier to see when the spider is shown against this speckled rock slab.

74

For years this species was called *Grammostola spatulata* or *Grammostola cala*, but apparently the present consensus is that *rosea* is the best name, at least for the time being. More changes may be expected, as the relationships of these tarantulas are not understood.

Brazilian Salmon
Lasiodora parahybana (Mello-Leitao 1917)

One of the largest species of tarantulas available, the Brazilian salmon has a leg span of 10 to 12 inches (25 to 30 cm) and a body length of about 4 inches (10 cm). This is a shaggy, dark brown to black spider that in females has a narrow pale rim across the front of the carapace. It inhabits burrows in moist rain forests of Brazil and thus needs a high relative humidity at all times, preferably about 70 to perhaps 80 percent, with a moist substrate for burrowing and a large water bowl. Adults have abdomens that are easily damaged, so they should not be allowed to climb—use a terrarium just a bit taller than they can reach when standing erect. This species can be aggressive and has a bad bite. It is not recommended for beginners and actually has little to recommend it other than its size.

Trinidad Chevron
Psalmopoeus cambridgei (Pocock 1895)

This fairly large (often more than 2.5 inches [6.3 cm]) tree-dwelling tarantula is easy to breed in captivity and thus quite available even though it comes from the small island of Trinidad off Venezuela. At first glance, it appears to be just a pale brown tarantula, but a closer look at the legs shows a more complicated pattern, including a distinctive orange spot on the foot with an orange line extending up the leg; there may be more orange lines on the knee and some spotting on the other segments. Because of its large size, it needs a tall terrarium (at least 16 inches [40 cm]), which soon will become coated with a layer of thick webbing. Though commonly kept, this can be a fast and quite aggressive spider, and some keepers have accused it of having a bad bite.

Goliath Pink-Foot
Pseudotheraphosa apophysis (Tinter 1991)

Adults of this giant species have a body 4 inches (10 cm) long and leg span of at least 13 inches (33 cm). They are from Venezuela and are virtually indistinguishable from the Goliath bird-eater (see below) except for the presence of pink feet in juveniles (lost in adults) and the fact that adult males have tibial apophyses (lacking in the Goliath bird-eater). Because of the minor nature of the differences, the genus *Pseudotheraphosa* now often is considered to be a synonym of *Theraphosa*, but remember that the taxonomy of these gigantic spiders still is not understood. This species also has some of the worst urticating hairs of any tarantula and can cause bleeding sores and serious respiratory problems in a susceptible keeper. Like other giants, it needs a high relative humidity and lots of moisture in the terrarium. This species is kept as a curiosity and is not recommended for beginners, even if it were affordable.

The pink on the toes of this giant species fades and sometimes disappears on adults such as the specimen shown here. The pink toes of young Goliath pinkfoots are quite bold and stand out against their brown or black bodies.

Goliath Bird-Eater
Theraphosa blondi (Latreille 1804)

Long reputed to be the world's largest spider, the Goliath bird-eater of the Amazon Basin actually shares that reputation today with other species of tropical South America, including some *Lasiodora* and *Pseudotheraphosa* species.

This Goliath bird-eater is only a juvenile. By adulthood, its leg span could reach 12 inches (30 cm).

All may reach about a foot (30 cm) in leg span and a weight of about 4 ounces (more than 100 grams), though individuals vary greatly in overall size. Adults have a nearly round cephalothorax and brown (not deep black) legs; their coloration is not impressive. Adding to the difficulties of keeping this species are its aggressive kicking of potent urticating hairs, need for a high humidity and a deep substrate for burrowing, plus a low terrarium to prevent fatal climbing accidents. It may have a very bad bite. Spiderlings may take six years or more to approach adulthood and males lack tibial apophyses. Though popular, expensive, and widely bred in captivity, this is another species that has little to offer other than size, and it is not recommended. (The species name until recently was *leblondi* due to a misreading of the original French description.)

Some Old World Tarantulas

As a rule, tarantulas from Africa and southern Asia (few species are commercially available from the Middle East and Australia) are more aggressive than American tarantulas, and several have been claimed (admittedly often on weak evidence) to have serious bites. Because they tend to be more expensive than American tarantulas and in many areas are available only as imported adults (though some are captive-bred in decent numbers), they perhaps should be considered more suitable for advanced keepers.

Curved-Horn
Ceratogyrus bechuanicus (Purcell 1897)

Spiders in this genus usually have a large, dark brown hump or horn over the center of the foveal groove. In this species, the horn points backward toward the abdomen. (In other species in the hobby, the horn points forward, or it is erect.) This is a 2-inch (5-cm) burrowing tarantula that is pale brown overall with a weakly and irregularly spotted abdomen and a shiny cephalothorax. It is found in a belt across northern South Africa and probably in adjacent countries, where it inhabits dry habitats. In the terrarium, it does well if given a large water dish and the humidity is allowed to drop to about 50 percent. Females produce just a hundred young in an egg case; it is commonly bred in captivity.

Burmese Mustard
Chilobrachys andersoni (Pocock 1895)

Only recently imported in small numbers, this southern Asian tarantula comes from moist rain forests and seems to do best when kept at a high relative humidity, with vermiculite and potting soil to burrow into and a large water bowl. The overall color is a dirty yellowish brown, and the leg segments are distinctly ringed in dirty white. Like other Asian tarantulas, it can be aggressive and difficult to maintain in good health. It has a 2-inch (5-cm) body length.

King Baboon
Citharischius crawshayi (Pocock 1900)

South Africans call their tarantulas baboon spiders, but Americans prefer to refer to almost all of them as just tarantulas. The epitome of an aggressive tarantula, the king baboon, a 3-inch (7.5-cm) burrowing tarantula from dry areas of southern Africa, is notorious for rearing on its hind legs and challenging any movement in or near its cage. It can back up this threat with a bad bite and definitely should not be handled. Adults are reddish brown without strong patterns, and in females the hind legs are distinctly thickened and bowed. If allowed to burrow deeply into the substrate, this spider will disappear and seldom be seen. Usually it is

A spider for only the most experienced keepers, the king baboon tarantula is especially aggressive and is likely to bite anything—or anyone—that approaches its burrow.

given a large retreat cover (which soon will be covered with webbing) on vermiculite and provided with a large water bowl. It does fine at moderate (60 percent) relative humidity, but the cage may have to be misted daily if your specimen seems to lurk around the water bowl all the time. Tall cages may cause deaths from falls. Spiderlings grow very slowly and often eat poorly, so wild-caught imports still are common in the hobby. Because of its aggressive attitude, this species cannot be recommended for beginners.

Cobalt Blue
Haplopelma lividum (A. Smith 1996)
This aggressive species from Thailand and Myanmar (Burma) is kept largely because of the bright colors of some females, which are brighter than males. Females may have an iridescent blue cephalothorax, blue lines on a blackish brown abdomen, a pink front edge of the carapace, and dull to

This cobalt blue tarantula's rich hue makes it one of the more desired species. It has an aggressive temperament and, therefore, is better suited for an experienced hobbyist.

iridescent blue legs. They do best when given a deep substrate of potting soil with vermiculite and when the ambient humidity is 70 percent or higher. Provide a large water bowl and watch the spider's behavior closely. This species has a bad bite and is not recommended for beginners even if the price drops significantly. It has a 2.5-inch (6.3-cm) body length.

Cameroon Red
Hysterocrates gigas (Pocock 1897)

Often mistakenly sold under the name *Hysterocrates hercules* (a different species, the Goliath baboon), this 3-inch (7.6-cm) tarantula from western Africa is a uniform dark brown with reddish bristles on the legs (of which the hind pair is enlarged) and few other distinctive features. Adults can be kept much like the king baboon, and—like the king baboon—Cameroon reds can be quite aggressive. One unusual behavior of this species is that its spiderlings can be kept together until they reach almost 2 inches (5 cm) in leg span with few instances of cannibalism. This means they can be reared several dozen at one time in a large covered container with an inch or so (2.5 cm) of vermiculite, potting soil, and sphagnum moss that is misted daily.

Sri Lankan Ornamental
Poecilotheria fasciata (Latreille 1804)

Among the most famous of the tree-dwelling tarantulas, the Sri Lankan ornamental also is one of the most beautiful. Males of this long-legged species are dusky brown with only indistinct patterns, but females have an elaborate gray pattern down the center of the abdomen, on the cephalothorax, and on the legs. In both sexes, the undersides of the first two legs and the pedipalps are spotted with bright yellow alternating with dark brown, a pattern designed to startle a predator when the legs are suddenly lifted off the substrate. This species grows to a 3-inch (7.6-cm) body length.

The several species of ornamental tarantulas from Sri Lanka and India all have similar patterns and similar lifestyles. They live in tree holes and similar retreats, building dense webs to help retain moisture during the dry season. They are extremely fast, may be aggressive, and have a bite that has been shown to be dangerous (though probably not deadly) to humans. As might be expected, they are expensive even when bred in captivity. Give ornamentals a tall terrarium with a moderate humidity level and a large water bowl; a substrate may not be necessary if they are allowed to climb a branch, a section of cork bark, or a partially hollowed out log.

Related to the Sri Lankan is the Indian ornamental tarantula (*Poecilotheria regalis*) which has darker and wider brown stripes across the top of the abdomen leading from the central grayish area, and often has more gray on the legs. Females have a pale brown bar across the abdomen under the epigastric ridge. It also differs from *P. fasciata* in that a dozen or so spiderlings can be raised together until they are almost grown, and even adult pairs can be left together—though deaths due to cannibalism are always possible. Like other ornamentals (there are several available species), these are aggressive and expensive spiders.

Mombasa Golden Starburst
Pterinochilus murinus (Pocock 1897)

This 2-inch (5-cm) tarantula from southeastern Africa is typical of a group of similar species or subspecies that vary somewhat in coloration and in details of structure; they may have been hybridized in the terrarium, unfortunately. The overall color of this popular species is a rich golden tan, with a few darker spots on the abdomen and some white bristles at the edges of the leg segments. The star-burst is a pattern of radiating whitish lines coming from the center of the foveal groove and contrasting with the golden brown carapace. There may be no truly bright colors, but this is a very pretty species. It is typical of relatively dry areas from Kenya to Zambia, and it does well in a simple terrarium setup with moderate relative humidity and a retreat (that is quickly covered with web-bing). Provide a large water bowl and watch the spider's behavior to see if more moisture is necessary: if the spider lingers by the water bowl, the terrarium is probably too

A top view of this Mombasa golden starburst tarantula shows its distinctive black, starburst pattern on the carapace.

dry; if the spider will not burrow and remains in the driest area of its enclosure, the substrate is too wet. Spiderlings may need more moisture than adults. This may be the only African tarantula that can be recommended for beginners, though it may be fairly aggressive and there has been at least one report of a bad reaction to a bite.

Feather-Leg
Stromatopelma calceatum (Pocock 1897)

One of the few tarantula species that definitely has been reported to cause hospitalization after its bite, this tree-dwelling species from western Africa is about 2.5 inches (6.3 cm) long. It is a pretty spider—the grayish body has a spotted and radiated pattern, and the dark gray legs have black spots on the outer segments. Long bristles on the leg segments give them a feathered look, thus, the common name. In nature, these spiders live in large numbers in palm plantations and are feared by the workers, perhaps with good reason. They are very fast, are good jumpers, and are very aggressive, so they cannot be recommended for beginners.

Summary

Obviously the two dozen or so species mentioned here represent just the tip of the iceberg when it comes to available tarantulas, and certainly a dedicated hobbyist could find another two or three dozen species with minimal stalking of the Internet. Beginners are again cautioned to start with common, inexpensive species that are not aggressive or have odd requirements and to learn their basics before moving to more complicated species.

CHAPTER 7

OTHER INTERESTING SPIDERS

Considering there are some thirty-five thousand species of spiders known (with many more still to be described), it should come as no surprise that tarantulas are not the only spiders of potential interest to terrarium keepers.

Trapdoor Spiders

Several families of nontheraphosid tarantulas are known for building burrows that they densely line with silk and then close with a round or oval door made from many layers of silk. The door may be hinged with silk at one side or at the center or held in place like a cork in a bottle. In either case, the tarantula tends to lurk just below the door, holding it in place with spines on the front legs, or chelicerae. When it recognizes the tread of a prey insect or if the prey thumps on a line of silk that serves as an alarm, the spider moves very rapidly to open the door, move out of the hole, grab the prey, drop back into the hole, and close the door again. This can happen literally in the blink of an eye.

Trapdoor spiders usually are found in dry, open, often rocky country, where large colonies of individuals may dig dozens of burrows in an area where the temperature, humidity, and soil conditions are just right. Often the entrance to the burrow is camouflaged by bits of twigs and gravel, and twigs may be glued onto the door with silk. Finding the burrow of a trapdoor spider can be virtually impossible until you spot one and you get an eye for seeing the others near it.

Shown here is a red trapdoor spider, possibly an *Idiops* species. This species comes from Africa.

Though many trapdoor spiders are small—less than an inch (2.5 cm)—a few common species may be from 1 to 2 inches (2.5 to 5 cm) in body length. As a rule, trapdoor spiders have smooth, shiny bodies and legs with just a few hairs, not the dense bristling of bird-eating tarantulas.

Most trapdoor spiders belong to the family Ctenizidae, which has several members in the southern United States, including *Bothriocyrtum californicum*, the Californian trapdoor spider, which is common on hillsides in parts of Southern California. After rains, adult males sometimes leave their burrows to visit females and may be found strolling through backyards. A few uncommon species of *Cyclocosmia*, which have the tip of the abdomen flattened into a hardened plate with a complicated arrangement of grooves and circles, are found in ravines of the southeastern United States and Mexico; they use the thickened abdominal plate to help plug the burrow. In the African Idiopidae, a pair of eyes is set on a separate tubercle in front of the other six eyes, giving these trapdoors their common name: front-eyed tarantulas. At least two species belonging to genus *Idiops* are available to hobbyists: one with blackish legs, and the other with glossy, reddish brown legs. Also in the hobby are members of the family Nemesiidae (mostly unidentified species) from Africa, Chile, and possibly southern Europe; these tend to be funnel-web builders rather than true trapdoor burrowers, building tight, circular, nearly horizontal webs under rocks and other cover.

Though they require deeper substrates into which they can burrow and more attention to the relative humidity near the bottom of the burrow, trapdoor spiders will do quite well in a terrarium with shallow substrate, just using a retreat cover and not trying to burrow, but this fails to give them the opportunity to show off their handiwork. Crickets and other insects are the major food.

Widow Spiders

The many species of genus *Latrodectus* are known as the widow spiders and are best known in the United States as the black widows. In this country, the common species have very large, rounded abdomens that bear a pattern of two red triangles (point to point) on the underside and commonly a line of small red spots down the top center. These are smooth spiders with only a few obvious bristles on the legs. Males are about half the length of females, with large females approaching half an inch (about 1.1 cm) in body length; males also are brightly colored with curved red lines on the sides and top of the abdomen. Exotic species of widow spiders are similar in shape but may have white patterns on the abdomen or be largely shades of brown.

Widow spiders are notorious for their toxic bite that is dangerous to humans, at least in theory. Species vary greatly in their toxicity, but the common U.S. species have indeed killed children in the past, though not in recent decades because an antivenin is now available. Their venom is one of the most deadly known, but fortunately it is injected in extremely small quantities, so it seldom produces more than minor symptoms (pain, sweating, difficulty in breathing due to tightness of the chest muscles and diaphragm) that pass in a few days under medical observation. Many bites produce no symptoms and are assumed to be "dry" (venomless) bites. If you are bitten by a widow spider, seek medical attention but don't panic—adults seldom have become even seriously ill as a consequence. Children, with their low body weight, may be in more immediate danger and may need antivenin.

Despite recent development of an antivenin to counteract the toxic venom of widow spiders such as this black widow, sight of these spiders is alarming for many people. There have been a few reported deaths related to widow spider bites, but in most cases the victims were children; the venom is more highly concentrated in a child's small body.

These spiders typically build open, very irregular webs and prey snares near the ground in a dark spots, such as under bark slabs or in the corners of outbuildings. There they feed on tiny insects. Males sometimes live in the corners of the females' webs and they may share food, though occasionally the males are eaten after mating. Most males survive mating, however, so the term *widow spider* is misleading. Keep these spiders (though dangerous, they can be collected or purchased in some areas) in small, dark containers that are relatively dry (50 percent humidity) and allow females to build webs. Fruit flies and pinhead crickets are good foods. The terraria of these spiders should be placed inside a larger cage that can be securely sealed and locked to prevent escapes and unauthorized entries.

Weavers and Silk Spiders

Some of the most beautiful spiders make up the family Araneidae, the orb weavers; they're noted for building large webs in trees and shrubs and on houses, each web consisting of several circles of silk and an elaborate system of sticky silk threads in the center. Though sometimes sold, they also are easily collected in the later summer, and they commonly live until the first frosts of autumn. Many species are half an inch (1.2 cm) long or more, with very long legs and

The marbled orb weaver (*Araneus marmoreus*), in its common form as shown here, is noted for its bold orange cephalothorax and orange and yellow abdomen. This nocturnal species is harmless to humans and usually is docile.

impressive color patterns on the oval or even sculptured abdomen. Often found in most parts of the United States are thornbacks (genera *Gasteracantha* and *Micrathena*), which have large, hard, thornlike spines on the abdomen; orchard spiders, (*Leucauge* spp.), which have a delicate silvery pattern; many species of garden spiders (*Argiope* spp.) with their relatively elongated abdomens bearing bright colors; and the confusing species of shamrock spiders (*Araneus* spp.), which have long bristles on the legs and rounded abdomens that often feature a pattern of yellow spots.

Sometimes seen on dealer lists are true silk spiders of genus *Nephila* spp., which includes several species from around the world in warm climates. Most are about an inch (2.5 cm) long, with long legs that bear cuffs of dense bristles around at least one set of joints on most legs. The abdomen is elongated and rather boxlike with distinctly flat sides, and usually has a pattern that includes several pairs of bright yellow spots against a tan to greenish background. One silk spider, *Nephila clavipes*, is common from the southeastern United States into the American tropics. It builds gigantic, finely woven webs between trees in moist lowland forests; the webs usually appear incomplete, as if missing a section, and the sticky threads in the center are yellow.

Many silk spiders and other orb weavers can be kept in a special thin terrarium between two panes of glass a foot (30 cm) or more square that are held apart by strips of wood about 2 inches (5 cm) wide. The whole terrarium is sealed around except for a screened hole at the top for adding food and water. These spiders also can be accommodated in gallon (3.8 L) jars and even in ordinary aquaria, where they will spin webs to fit the container. They seldom come to the ground and should be lightly misted daily (excessive water may break the webs), and fed on fruit flies and similar insects. Some orb weavers tear down their webs each evening and build new ones each night. These are considered intelligent spiders with many interesting behavior patterns.

Jumping Spiders

Perhaps the most intelligent spiders, or at least the ones with the most personality, are the solitary hunters belonging to the family Salticidae, the jumping spiders. These can be seen walking in the sun along tree trunks and along the sides of buildings during much of the year and throughout the world. The family is composed of dozens of confusing genera and hundreds of species. Males often have much brighter patterns than females have, including areas of iridescent red, green, blue, or yellow scales (flattened bristles) on the front legs that they use to attract females. The central pair of eyes is greatly enlarged and looks forward, giving them binocular vision; they also can see colors and apparently can discriminate between subjects viewed at considerable distance. They run quickly, jump

With approximately four thousand members in the jumping spider family (Salticidae), the most common species, shown here, is the daring jumping spider (*Phidippus audax*).

well (generally attaching a safety line of fine silk to one spot before jumping into space to another), and don't seem to be afraid of humans. I often have one or two males of *Phidippus audax* (black with a large white spot on the center of the upper abdomen) or a similar species visiting the computer while I write, apparently interested in what I'm doing. (Okay, I exaggerate—I don't really know if they are interested, but they seldom seem bored.) Most common jumping spiders are a quarter inch to half an inch in length (6.3 to 12.7 mm), but they are heavy-bodied and seem larger.

Jumping spiders feed on small insects of all types, and they can be kept in small containers with minimal substrate and a surface or two on which to bask. They have no fear of sunlight, but make sure their terraria do not get much warmer than 90°F (32.2°C); the humidity should be relatively low. It's actually more fun to watch wild jumping spiders than ones kept in captivity. They have fascinating courtship rituals, including the male offering food to the female.

Wolf Spiders

The wolf spiders, family Lycosidae, are responsible for the word *tarantula*. During the Middle Ages, this term was applied to several European wolf spiders that were said to cause wild dancing as a side-effect of their bite. The dancing (accompanied by equally rapid music) known as a tarantella, was said to be the only cure for the venomous bite of these small spiders. Actually, the dancing and music were probably mass distractions used to escape the very static, confining life of the Middle Ages, and wolf spiders are no more venomous than other spiders—their bite certainly does not induce dancing (maybe some hopping about and cursing, but not dancing). There are many types of wolf spiders, ranging up to about an inch (2.5 cm) in length, with moderately long legs that bear only a few long bristles. The abdomen is large, and the female usually attaches the round white egg case to the spinnerets and carries it around with her; spiderlings may ride on top of the mother for several days until they go their own way. Identification of wolf spiders is complex; there are species found from the sides of

This wolf spider's black and brown body pattern helps it easily blend in with its surroundings. Wolf spiders build highly camouflaged retreats and have been known to capture prey much larger than their 1-inch (2.5-cm) bodies, such as frogs and lizards, although they mainly eat insects and other spiders.

streams to the centers of deserts, and many live under litter and debris in open woods and near houses. Most species are grayish to brownish with a pair of darker stripes running down the entire body; some have deep black undersides. A few species from dry habitats even build short burrows and cap them with a corklike silken trap door.

Wolf spiders are active hunters that run down their prey from camouflaged hiding places. They are quick movers, and American species have a painful (though harmless) bite with which they take quite large prey. Some wolf spiders under an inch (2.5 cm) long have been noted to attack and kill frogs, lizards, and even shrews. The larger species can be kept much like tarantulas (which they are sometimes mistaken for by many laypeople in the northern United States where wolf spiders are abundant) but they generally need less humidity. These spiders can be very difficult to corner and move from one spot to another—be careful.

Summary

Numerous other interesting spiders can be found near almost any home in the United States, and some are large enough to consider keeping as temporary pets in jars or plastic boxes of the appropriate size. Most will accept a substrate of vermiculite or vermiculite and potting soil, will eat insects, and will live a few weeks or months before dying naturally. Most spiders are short-lived, which reduces their desirability as pets, but they certainly can be fun to observe.

RESOURCES

Societies

American Arachnological Society
A scientific society devoted to all arachnids.
c/o Dr. J. W. Schultz
Department of Entomology
University of Maryland
College Park, MD 20742
On the Web at: http://www.americanarachnology.org
Publishes *Journal of Arachnology*

American Tarantula Society
P.O. Box 756
Carlsbad, NM 88221-0756
On the Web at: http://www.atshq.org
Publishes *The Forum Magazine*

Web Sites

http://www.tarantulas.com
A very large site with many links and postings by dealers and hobbyists.

http://www.exoticpets.about.com/cs/tarantulas/a/
tarantulasaspets4.htm
The tarantula pages of this multipet site include care sheets for several common species, a variety of links, and some archived articles on general care and breeding.

http://research.amnh.org/invertzoo/catalogues.html
This is *The World Spider Catalog* by Dr. Norman Platnick of the American Museum of Natural History. A highly technical literature compilation, it contains an up-to-date, extensive bibliography and lists of synonyms.

INDEX

ABOUT THE AUTHOR

A native of central Louisiana, **Jerry Walls** worked as an editor in New Jersey for more than thirty years, authoring more than four hundred publications on natural history subjects, especially reptiles and amphibians. His thirty-eight books (including twenty on herps) range from introductory works on lizards and turtles as pets to massive reviews of seashells, boas and pythons, and poisonous frogs. He also edited *Reptile Hobbyist* magazine and currently writes a monthly column for *Reptiles* magazine. He is an active birder, with more than six hundred U.S. species on his life list, and has authored several books and articles on pet and wild birds. Collecting crawfishes, snails, and herps for taxonomic study currently is his favorite preoccupation.